THE LOVE WE KNEW

A True Story of Love, Loss, and Reunion

JOHN R. GAMMINO

JRA
PUBLISHING, LLC
Vero Beach, Florida

THE LOVE WE KNEW
A True Story of Love, Loss, and Reunion

For information, contact:
JRA Publishing, LLC
johngammino.com

Hardcover ISBN: 978-1-7374901-1-1
Paperback ISBN: 978-1-7374901-0-4
Library of Congress Control Number: 2021912922

To my lovely wife, Pat,
who gave life, encouragement and support
to our extended family.

Our lives are forever enriched from the
legacy of love that you left behind.

I remember good times
and relive the sad
The laughter, the love,
the good and the bad
I remember all the things
We used to do
Pausing to replay
the love that we knew

– from the song, "The Love We Knew,"
lyrics by John R. Gammino, music by Ryan Reeson

CONTENTS

ACKNOWLEDGMENTS

With thanks to the following:

Pat, who with energetic spirit, motherly leadership and encompassing love provided the impetus for this story to be told.

Lisa, Maureen, Melissa and Mike, who assisted in keeping the story focused and who refreshed my recollections of events.

Jim and Gina, my brother and sister-in-law, who provided so many laughs and such joy to Pat over the years and whose support of me has been steadfast since Pat has been gone. Jim also contributed a story from his son that captured Pat's caring heart.

Our community of friends in Vero Beach, who gave so unselfishly of their time and energy to support our family during Pat's final months.

Tracey Timpanaro, whose talents, insights and tireless work ethic were invaluable in the writing and editing of this story.

Ella Ritchie and the staff of Stellar Communications Houston, who provided exceptional, professional support services and who facilitated the organization and completion of *The Love We Knew*.

INTRODUCTION

⁓

Writing a book is not an undertaking for the faint of heart. It requires an inordinate amount of hard work and discipline. So why did I do it? Mostly to honor my dear wife Pat and the incredible 63 years we spent together. But I also wanted to share our story as a way of making a contribution to the connection that is humankind. We all have these amazing tales that we accumulate as we navigate the myriad of trials and triumphs life has to offer, and life is always enriched when we share these experiences.

Pat and I met in seventh grade, and we were head over heels with each other straight away. I describe our journey through the ups and downs of life and the transformation of our relationship from its puppy-love beginning to a more mature version that featured heartfelt compromises, mutual admiration and support.

We were two kids from a small industrial town in New Jersey, but our story likely mirrored others in small towns all over the world. The experiences our generation had growing up could have been pulled from famous movies of the time: *Grease, Saturday Night Fever* and *Splendor in the Grass*. Our journey produced moments of tenderness and laughter as well as disappointment and sadness. We made substantial sacrifices for each other and for the good of our family.

Those of you who remember Dick Clark's *American Band-stand* will understand how fantastic it was for Pat and me to attend exuberant dance parties that drew 2,000 kids to Notre Dame High School in Bethlehem, Pennsylvania on Saturday nights. The stars of the famous TV show would attend, and the immensely popular DJ Gene Kaye would always wow the crowd.

Motivated kids of our generation strived to accomplish great things. High school sports provided the opportunity for many to achieve college scholarships and move on to successful careers. For most of us, life in the '50s and '60s was simpler in many ways. Over time, though, life presented challenges that tested us to our very core; I'm sure many of you experienced the same. As you follow us through the years, it is my hope that you are not only entertained, but that the culture and events described herein will trigger some of your own memories.

I have been asked frequently why I wrote this book in the third person. The answer is that I wanted this to be a story about our family and not just me. I wanted to step outside the tale and relay it as accurately as possible. In my mind, it is a lovely family narrative in which I am but one character. There are countless other stories that could have been included, but I did the best I could in choosing those I thought were representative of our lives together.

It has been challenging to convert actual experiences into words that can accurately relay the feelings of those who lived the events. In the end, I hope I have done the story justice. The love Pat and I shared with each other and with our family will live in my heart for the rest of my days. I wish the very same for each of you.

CHAPTER I

The Encounter

HE WAS STANDING AT THE BLACKBOARD. HIS name was John, but his friends called him Butch. Dressed in a plaid sport coat, white shirt and tie, he looked handsome and older than a 12-year-old, seventh-grade student. His hair was combed from left to right in a flawless manner. Sister Esther (of the Sisters of Mercy order) was asking questions of her class, and he was recording the responses. The good sister wanted him to break out of his shyness and learn to be the leader she sensed he would become. She made him president of the science class.

Suddenly, the door opened and a young girl came into the room. Butch stole a quick glance at her as she delivered a note to Sister Esther. She was dressed in a navy blue uniform, with a neatly starched white blouse and blue flats. Her green eyes lit up the room, and her brown hair was perfectly in place. In short, she was beautiful and he was instantly in love. There was something special about this girl. He had never laid eyes on her before, but he knew he must get to know her. And this is how their story begins—in a small Catholic school in the small town of Phillipsburg, New Jersey. The year was 1955.

Her name was Patricia, and he decided he would find a way to casually meet her. One day in the schoolyard at lunchtime, he walked up and introduced himself. He was usually bashful and nervous about relationships with girls other than simple friendships. But with this girl, it was different. She was new to the school and had attended a public school the year prior. He felt instantly comfortable talking with her. As he got to know her better, he would often walk her home from school. She lived on one of the two big hills in town. He lived on the other. The walk to her house and then to his was almost 3 miles, but he never noticed the distance. They would talk and laugh as they both told stories of their days. Pat's father was part owner of a butcher shop known as Morello's Meat Market. Butch's father was a detective with the police force. Both Pat and Butch were happy kids who had no idea they were poor.

When classmates from Phillipsburg Catholic had birthday parties, Butch always made sure Pat was invited. She didn't know all the kids in the school the way he did; he had been with most of them since kindergarten.

For such a young group of Catholic school kids, there were an inordinate number of parties. Pat and Butch were together a lot. The parties were quite fun; the kids would dance to rock-and-roll records and of course would play spin the bottle. The "winners" would go into a closet or a private area in the room and kiss. It was like being sent to the electric chair or eating a delicious piece of chocolate cake. There wasn't much in between. You loved the experience or you hated it! Naturally, there were the favorites, but if the bottle didn't point to them, you couldn't make a face or show your displeasure, because that would be rude.

As time passed and eighth grade came along, Butch bought a friendship ring for Pat. The ring was a sign of their special relationship. They were officially boyfriend and girlfriend. At parties, spin the bottle gave way to "flashlight." In this game, you tried to catch a couple kissing in the dark. If you shined the light on them and caught them, then one of them became the flashlight holder.

This group of socially active young people was very special. There were more than 100 kids who were together until high school, and Pat and Butch were an "item" all throughout. They broke up and got back together multiple times; teenage hormones were clearly to blame. Pat dated guys from the public high school at times. Butch was jealous. Butch dated girls from the public high school at times. Pat was jealous. By the time they were well into their sophomore year, they both realized the attraction they felt for each other was a deep and abiding love. Even then, neither could have predicted the emotional and challenging times that were in store—and the love story that would emerge as a legacy.

CHAPTER 2

Teenagers in Love

LONG BEFORE BUTCH MET PAT, HE PLAYED QUAR-terback on the Pop Warner Police Athletic League (PAL) team. In 1953, when he was 9 years old, the town paid for the team to go to Miami to play in the first Junior Orange Bowl game. Volunteers in the Fort Lauderdale area were solicited to house the young players during their stay in Florida. Butch and teammate Danny Myers were paired with a wealthy family. There were Cadillacs in the driveway, a basketball court, and a stream behind the house with what seemed like flying fish.

Butch was very uncomfortable and very impressed at the same time. The first night at dinner, they were seated around a large dining room table. The man of the house pressed a button with his foot, and the maid began bringing dinner from the kitchen to the dining room. Butch had never experienced such wealth. He lived in a small home that had been built as temporary housing for returning veterans. It was very basic, and when they moved in, there were no sidewalks or paved streets. That did change over time, but the surroundings were humble at best.

The Junior Orange Bowl game was played in the Orange Bowl Stadium in Miami, and the PAL team won. The kids were ecstatic beyond belief. The team was taken to see the college Orange Bowl game a couple of days later between Maryland and Oklahoma. The entire experience was fantastic for the impressionable youngsters.

Each year thereafter, the team won additional championships and traveled to distant locations to play in major events. Eventually, Pat entered the picture, and she played the role of supportive girlfriend very well. For example, when the young couple was in eighth grade, each was weighed and measured at school. Butch was 5 feet, 2 inches tall and weighed 102 pounds. Pat was 5 feet, 2½ inches tall and weighed 105 pounds. However, Pat told him she weighed 100 so as not to make him feel bad.

As a freshman in high school, Butch was on the varsity football team. The few times he got into games, he was able to create exciting pass plays that resulted in several touchdowns. By sophomore year, he was the starting quarterback and was well known as a great passer. After each game, the high school girls would line up outside the field house where the players showered and changed back into street clothes. The throng of girls would cheer them as they came out the door. It was an exciting time. Then the football players and their girlfriends would often go out for something to eat.

If it was a night game, they would often go "parking." Parking may be a lost term these days, but back then, it meant you were going to make out with your partner. Some called it "watching the submarine races." Because Butch and Pat were so attracted to each other, these were very special moments when they could find a secluded spot and show their affection and love. It wasn't total privacy because neither Butch nor Pat had their driver's license, so they would go with other couples.

On one such occasion, Pat and Butch were out with friends who sometimes went parking at Mount Parnassus. It was a remote place in town by the Delaware River, with two large and desolate hills. While the two couples were talking, Pat said that she thought she'd heard something. That led to a discussion of an infamous folk story about a man who had a hook for a hand. As the story went, the hookman was about to enter a car in which two kids were passionately making love. One was startled by a noise. The driver took off, and when he reached his girlfriend's house and got out of the car, there was a hook attached to the driver's side door handle. No one knew if the story was real, but it was so frightening that the kids quickly drove off.

The next day, Butch's father, Jake, came home for lunch, as he often did when he worked on Sundays. He was a detective in the police department. He mentioned that he had a poisonous rash on his arms, so Butch asked how that happened. His dad said that he had spent the morning walking through the brush and woods on Mount Parnassus with some other policemen, because an escapee from a nearby prison was rumored to have been hiding there the previous night. Butch tried to be cool, although he felt his heart would pop out of his chest. Shortly thereafter, he excused himself from the table. He went into the bathroom to take some slow, deep breaths and collect his thoughts. His strategy worked, for when he returned, neither parent knew that he had been so upset.

In his junior year, Butch was 5 feet, 11 inches tall and weighed 175 pounds. He was no longer shorter or skinnier than Pat, whose measurements remained the same. Even though they lost a few close games during the season, Butch led the team to a state championship among Catholic high schools.

The following summer was a very special time. The soon-to-be senior football players got together each evening after work to train. They repeated running, sprinting, calisthenics and passing drills over and over in an effort to be the best that they could be. The backfield was made up entirely of seniors. They got their hands on the Iowa University playbook. They used it to rehearse inside reverses, pass-run options and other college-level offensive plays. The four offensive backs practiced with precision. They worked hard and were devoted to being undefeated in the season ahead. They also shared the playbook with their coach so that he could prepare the offensive line for the same set of plays.

That summer was special for another reason. It was the first time that Pat and Butch would consummate their love. During their previous years together, they had done everything but allow their love to result in sex. As innocent kids, they explored exciting ventures into love. One night they went for a stroll in a park not far from Pat's house, and their bodies shared a sacred bond for the very first time. From that day on, they could not wait to be together.

Meanwhile, football season was approaching, and the team was ready. This bunch of poor kids from a small Catholic school would go into the basement of the school, which doubled as both a locker room and a cafeteria, and don their football uniforms. The school didn't have its own field, so practices were held in the local public park. To get to Walters Park, the team had to walk several blocks to a railroad overpass, climb a steep hill, and walk for a mile on the railroad tracks to the practice field. When practice was finished, they did the same in reverse. It was a pretty exhausting routine, so to be on this team was special. It required commitment. It was its own kind of American dream. Motivation was abundant, and these kids were driven to be winners.

There were several weeks of formal practice before the first game. A practice game was arranged with a team from Rockaway Township. When the two teams met, the Rockaway

*Pat and Butch attended many school dances together, including
their senior prom in May of 1961.*

team chuckled at how small the Catholic Terriers were in
comparison to their huge line. However, the Catholic team
had the last laugh. Butch was a smart play caller, and the
coach gave him great latitude. Catholic essentially schooled
their opponents repeatedly until they had whipped the big guys
badly. It was pretty sweet justice given the initial arrogance
of the other team. Needless to say, the Terriers were ready for
the season!

Word of the Terriers' prowess spread, and one team even
deflated footballs before a game to thwart Butch's passing attack.

The strategy didn't work. The team racked up nine straight wins in an unbeaten and untied football season. Many players on the team were recognized with awards. Butch received the Scholar Athlete award for the Lehigh Valley region and was honored at a dinner celebration. He had become a very public figure, and his picture was in the paper numerous times. He was an invited guest on local radio shows. Scouts from several colleges came to the school to see if there were prospects for scholarships. Several were awarded. Butch won a scholarship to Notre Dame, which led to even more publicity. Notre Dame arranged for Butch to redshirt for a year at the Bullis School in Silver Spring, Maryland. Things were progressing in storybook fashion, and Butch was humble yet proud of his accomplishments.

Butch and Pat were favorites of the nuns, but they didn't always know that. Pat could imitate her typing teacher, Sister Reparata, with precision. She would say in a nasally voice: "It certainly is well for you, Miss Morello, that you can talk in class when you should be working on your typing assignment." The football coach, who also taught health, spoke with a lisp, and Pat could imitate him perfectly. She would pound her ring on the desk and say with a lisp: "If you keep it down, class, I will pass all of you." She didn't do it in a mocking way, but rather in a very humorous way and never in their presence.

It was the sixties, and the kids grew up dancing. In high school, lunch break was known as "noon recreation." A record player was brought out each day, and students would dance in the auditorium. Dancing was a big part of life in the sixties.

Life was good at this small Catholic high school, and many great friendships were formed, including some that would last a lifetime. But in just a few months, everything would change for Pat and Butch.

Thirty-five years later, John and Pat visited some of the nuns who taught them, including Sister Yvonne, Sister Denise, Sister Theophane, and Sister Reparata, who Pat didn't think liked her. To her surprise, Sister Reparata put her arm around Pat and said, "You were my favorite. I didn't want the class to know!" Sister could not stop laughing as Pat rendered an imitation of sister's admonishments in class.

CHAPTER 3

The Surprise

PAT GOT HER DRIVER'S LICENSE BEFORE BUTCH did, and she learned to drive in her mother's 1953 Buick. It was a very big car, as many were in those days. Pat's mom, Ina Morello, taught her daughter how to drive. The Morellos had a detached garage a short distance from the house. One day Pat thought she could put the car away for her mother, but she didn't quite judge the distances properly. The Buick's bumper hit the side of the garage. Pat said to her mother, "Somehow the garage moved." Her sense of humor was lost on Ina, who was not happy about the situation. Fortunately, the damage to the garage was minimal and there was no visible damage to the car.

Butch took his driving test in December. He passed with no problem, but he was concerned about the color test because he was colorblind. The tester turned on a light and asked Butch the color.

Butch said, "White." He saw the look on the guy's face and quickly said, "Green."

The guy looked askance at Butch.

He then flashed another color and Butch said, "Red?"

The instructor gave him another quizzical look but said "Merry Christmas."

Butch was very happy to be a legal driver. Having a license did not necessarily mean that you had wheels. In those days, the wheels belonged to the parents. You had to borrow your parent's car unless you were one of the few that managed to buy an old jalopy and pay for the gas and maintenance. Butch was lucky because he was able to use his father's car quite often. In return, he would wash the car each weekend after mowing the grass and polishing his father's shoes and his own.

In those days, the happening place to be on the weekends was Notre Dame High School in Bethlehem, Pennsylvania. More than 2,000 kids would come and pay a dollar to go to the biggest dance party on the East Coast (and perhaps the country). Many of the major stars who were on Dick Clark's *American Bandstand* would come to Notre Dame on Saturday night. It was always an absolute blast. Pat and Butch went to these dances every Saturday night, as did many of their friends.

After a night of dancing and socializing with friends from the area, the kids would head out for a Philly steak sandwich at Joe's Steak Shop or a pizza at Colonial Tavern in Easton. Afterward, it was time for the parking to begin. It was the stuff of movies—definitely hot and heavy. *Grease, Saturday Night Fever,* and other movies portrayed the '50s and the '60s beautifully.

In April of 1961, life was pretty sweet for Butch and Pat, but then one day the bottom fell out.

Pat wasn't feeling well, so her mother took her to the doctor. The doctor ran some tests, and the results showed that Pat was pregnant. When Pat called Butch, he heard the nervousness in her voice. She said that her mother wanted him to come by to speak with her.

She then said, "I'm pregnant."

Two 17-year-olds were thrown into complete disarray. Everything had been perfect. *How could this be happening? Why is this happening? What are we going to do?* All of these thoughts raced through their minds. Butch and Pat contemplated running away and getting married. They were both 17, soon to be 18. However, to be considered an adult in those days, you had to be 21. Otherwise, you were required to get parental permission for an early marriage. That was *not* going to happen. They didn't have any money and had no means of transportation to escape the little town.

In short, they were stuck.

CHAPTER 4

The Emotional Roller Coaster

BUTCH'S FATHER, JAKE, WAS NOW THE TOWN clerk. Earlier in his career, Jake had been the first Italian on the police force in Phillipsburg, and he was conscious of how he was breaking through barriers for other Italian Americans. At that time, however, in a predominantly Irish town, there was much disdain for the Italians, and some of it was directed at Jake. Nonetheless, Jake did everything he could to be an exemplary policeman.

Every day when Jake finished his beat, he walked back to police headquarters. In doing so, he had to pass a restaurant where locals would be gathered outside smoking. For several days, as Jake passed, one guy would say, "There goes the guinea cop." Jake tried his best to ignore the comments so as not to make a scene, but then the day came when he'd had enough. When the slur was made, Jake grabbed the man by the throat, lifted him in the air and said, "From now on when I pass you, you will say, 'Good morning, Officer Gammino.' Do you understand?" The choking man assured

Jake that he understood. From that day on, Jake received his respectful greeting.

Jake and Rose raised their two sons to be Americans. Even though they spoke Italian—sometimes to avoid letting the boys know the content of their conversations—the boys were not taught Italian. Jake was tough on the boys in some ways and lenient in others. He coached their baseball teams and took them fishing all the time. But, above all, Jake wanted no embarrassments to the reputation that he had worked so hard to establish.

Pat's mother called Jake to tell him the news that Pat was pregnant. Jake went ballistic. He chastised Butch and said Butch had taken 10 years off his life. He told Butch about how hard he had worked to establish his good reputation and how Butch had ruined it. It was an ugly scene for Butch, but ultimately it became uglier for Pat.

Both sets of parents met multiple times to discuss the situation. Ina lobbied hard for Butch to go to a local college and for them to be married. However, Jake was very strong-willed and adamant that Pat should go away to have the baby, and that the baby would be given to a Catholic adoption agency. Essentially, he limited the options to just that one.

Graduation was in June. A neighbor of the Morellos had friends in Attica, New York, who agreed to take Pat in. She wasn't due until December, so she was able to hide her pregnancy with girdles and loose clothing. During the months of June and July, Butch was permitted to see her with supervision.

He visited Pat at her house just before she was to go to Attica. The couple was extremely upset. They were so deeply in love, and both so very afraid of what lay ahead. They knew it was the last time they would see each other for months. Pat was going to an unknown place to stay with unknown people far away from her family and friends. Butch faced the exact same scenario. However, both were determined to get through their separation and reunite at Christmas time.

Pat left for Attica, where she was to stay until the baby arrived. Butch went on to the Bullis Academy in Silver Spring, Maryland. The cover story was that Jake had forced them to break up their relationship so that Butch could concentrate on college and his scholarship to Notre Dame. Rumors abounded in the small town, and it was an exceptionally difficult time for Pat and Butch and their families.

Pat was absolutely miserable in Attica. Incredibly, the people she stayed with were not friendly to her. They offered her little in the way of food and drink. They were totally detached and showed her no compassion, despite the fact that they were being compensated for letting her stay there. Pat was frightened, alone and seemingly unwelcome, not to mention having to go through all the trials of pregnancy by herself at such a young age.

One day Pat met Neva, who was a neighbor of the people with whom she was staying. She explained her situation to Neva. Neva befriended her, and she and her husband Vic welcomed Pat with open arms. She ended up spending most of her time in their home. Pat was eternally grateful and found comfort in the care and hospitality they showed her. Neva went for walks with Pat so the young mother-to-be would get some exercise.

Pat was in Attica from August until December. She was desperately homesick, and she missed her parents and friends. Most of all she missed her boyfriend, Butch.

When at Bullis, Butch lost his nickname and became "John" to the people he met. John focused hard on football, but Bullis was a difficult environment for him. It was a semi-military academy with a very rigid routine. He was up at 7 a.m. Shower and breakfast followed. Inspection of the room occurred at 8 a.m. Classes were from 8:30 a.m. to 3 p.m. with a 45-minute break for lunch. He had football practice from 3:30 to 5:30 every day. Dinner was at 6 and mandatory study was from 7 to 11. Lights out occurred at 11:15. The regimen was very grueling for him.

John was second in line at Bullis, behind a quarterback who was from the Virginia Military Institute, a college team (he had been dropped down to redshirt for a year). He was bigger and taller than John, but John was determined to become the starting quarterback. Because he had his heart set on Notre Dame, John knew he had to be the starter for Bullis so he would gain the recognition he needed to achieve his ultimate goal.

He worked hard at both his studies and football. When he contracted a cold, he continued to work as though it were nothing. That led to bronchitis, which didn't stop him. Eventually, he drove himself into pneumonia and had to spend more than a week in a military hospital. He became weak and pale and lost 10 pounds. Rose, Jake, and his brother, Jim, came to see him. It was a long four-hour drive for them.

When John was released from the hospital, he was more determined than ever and began the process of regaining his strength and competing for the starting quarterback position again. He started the second half of the game against the freshman team of the University of Delaware. John's performance in that game was better than expected. The following week there was a home game against Newport News Academy. This was a four-year college playing a prep school team. John had never been more ready for a game. He had become the starting quarterback and threw three touchdown passes. He completed 22 of 24 passes for 320 yards.

He became a kind of hero of Bullis Academy after that game. The entire school was buzzing about the game and John's performance. Anticipation was great for the next game against the Naval Academy. It seemed that John was progressing well. He had recovered from pneumonia, and his grades were getting better because he felt better and had had time to grow accustomed to the arduous schedule. His confidence as a quarterback was improving. But there was one unseen and unsettling emotion that he hid from his peers: He was deeply in love with a young woman he was forbidden to see.

The Navy game finally arrived. Bullis had 22 players. Most played both offense and defense. Navy, on the other hand, had more than twice the manpower, according to John's brother Jim, who attended the game with Rose and Jake. Bullis was outmanned and outgunned. However, the Bullis offense was formidable. Among the star players was Bill Hanley, an All-American high school tackle. Bob Winsor was a 6-foot-4-inch offensive back. Howard Smith was a 6-foot-3-inch wide receiver. Steve Shrader was an agile and elusive running back that could make most defenders wonder where their jockstrap was left. All the players were high school stars.

John entered the game with Bullis on their own 20-yard line, but he led the team to a touchdown. Bullis was up 6-0; the kicker missed the extra point. The game was close until the third quarter, but the Bullis team was getting tired, the Navy team was fresh because it could replace its tired players. Navy ended up winning 20-6, but the Bullis fans were proud of their team. The quarterback for Navy was a guy named Roger Staubach, who would end up in the NFL's Hall of Fame.

Although John was consumed with football and had achieved his goal of becoming the starting quarterback, he missed Pat terribly. There were occasional phone calls from the payphone at Bullis, but there was a major emptiness that accompanied his achievements on the football field.

On December 13, 1961, Pat gave birth to a little girl and named her Patti. She called John to tell him, and they both cried on the phone because they missed each other so much. She had had such a rough time in Attica, a young girl in a delicate condition so far from home with no one she knew to talk to or spend time with. She would later tell John of how lonely she'd been and how Vic and Neva made her stay more tolerable.

Back in Phillipsburg, rumors continued about whether Pat had gone away to have a baby. Fights broke out among some of John's friends who defended Pat and him against the onslaught of unkind words and comments.

Eventually, Christmas vacation arrived. Pat came home from Attica with her baby. Ina called Jake to ask if John wanted to come and see Patti. Once more, Jake came completely unglued. He called Ina deceitful and told her she had agreed to give the baby up for adoption. It was once again an ugly scene. He later forced John to call Pat in his presence and say that he would no longer see her or date her. John was humiliated and intimidated by his father. He was barely 18 years old and without legal authority to be on his own—an option he would likely have taken had it been his decision to make.

He went back to Bullis without seeing Pat or the baby, and he was pretty distressed. He was outwardly confident, but on the inside he felt emotionally sick. During the succeeding weeks, Pat started dating other guys who were only too eager to jump into the void left behind by John. She was beautiful in every way. She had proposals of marriage, but she declined them. Pat felt a trauma similar to what John was feeling. When she was forced to give her baby up for adoption, she was sobbing and literally could not hand Patti to the nun at the Catholic agency. The nun had to take Patti from her arms. She was distraught at having to part with the child that she had carried for nine months and had nurtured for several more. She was devastated beyond anything she could articulate.

John wasn't faring much better. One night at Bullis, he totally lost it. His roommate, Floyd Koch, could hear John sobbing in the bottom bunk. He asked what was wrong, and John broke down and told him the story. He missed Pat so much and was upset at how he had followed his father's orders. He felt emasculated. He thought he was going to lose her to someone else who lived in the town, who could influence her to marry. Floyd was so taken by the story that he wrote Pat a letter telling her of John's feelings for her and his remorse about following his father's orders.

John came home for a weekend and said he was going to a dance at Easton High School with a friend. As they were driving, John's friend saw a car that he thought was following them. John turned around to look and was sure it was his father's car. He told his friend to forget about the dance and take him home. He wanted to beat his dad to the house, which he did. John walked in and asked his mother where his father was. She said he was out. John asked, "Out where?" She didn't know what to say. Jake came in the door as they were talking, and John was no longer the subservient 18-year-old. He confronted his dad and said he knew that he had been following him. John said he would no longer be treated as a criminal by his father. Words got heated, and Jim, John's younger brother who was 12 at the time, got between them and told his dad to back off.

John went back to Bullis without seeing Pat. They wrote to each other, and John told her he wanted to see her the next time he came home. She agreed. The next weekend, John hitchhiked four and a half hours to Phillipsburg. When he arrived, he asked his dad if he could borrow the car. Surprisingly, Jake agreed. John drove straight to Pat's house, and that was the beginning of a secret romance.

CHAPTER 5

The Early Collegiate Years

AFTER THE BULLIS FOOTBALL SEASON WAS OVER, many colleges tried to recruit John. Among them was Colgate University. Tom Parnell of Colgate paid a visit to John's parents when John was home for the weekend. Tom told them that Colgate was prepared to offer John an academic scholarship, which would cover all four years of college, including tuition, room and board. He told them that if John got hurt playing football, he could keep his scholarship because Colgate was not allowed to give athletic scholarships. He went over all the details and did his best to convince Rose and Jake that John would fit in well at Colgate. John had visited Colgate as a senior in high school, but he had not been accepted there. He was amazed at what one year at Bullis had accomplished. John got offers from several universities and military academies that had rejected him when he was in high school. It was flattering, but his heart was set on going to Notre Dame.

Parnell sent a letter with the scholarship offer and set a deadline for a response. That deadline was Friday, April 27, 1962.

As the deadline approached, John had not yet heard from Notre Dame. Jake was afraid that if Notre Dame didn't come through, John would lose out on the Colgate opportunity. John accepted the Colgate scholarship on the Friday deadline.

The following Monday morning, a special delivery airmail letter arrived from Notre Dame offering John a full scholarship. Ironically, it had been written one day before the day he accepted the Colgate scholarship.

John was absolutely anguished over the situation. He wanted to renege on the Colgate offer and accept the Notre Dame offer. Jake said that John had to keep his word and go to Colgate. They argued about it. Jake said he was concerned that Notre Dame would rescind its scholarship if it found out about John's "situation" with Pat. Eventually, he convinced John to honor the Colgate commitment. It was over. John was not going to the school of his dreams. It was Jake's way or the highway, which was a pretty miserable place for John to be, but again, it was just the way of the world in those days. You did *not* question your parents' authority.

That summer, John's cousin was getting married, and the entire family on his mother's side attended. There were hundreds of people at the wedding; John had 31 first cousins. His Aunt Clara (his mother Rose's sister), who knew of John's love for Pat, confronted Rose and Jake at the reception and told them they shouldn't try to keep the two apart any longer. She was very convincing, because shortly thereafter Rose said to John, "You can bring Pat to the reception." John called Pat, not knowing whether she would agree to come, but she did. John left the festivities and went straight to Pat's house. They missed an hour or so of the reception, but there was plenty of celebration left. Pat had rushed to get ready and was very nervous, but she looked gorgeous. The entire family was happy to see Pat and John together. Rose and Jake seemed to have realized that the inevitable was occurring with or without their consent.

John had graduated from Bullis Academy with excellent grades, and he had made some wonderful friends. Little did he know that he would never see most of them again. He worked very hard over the summer to get ready for the freshman season at Colgate. He and Pat were now openly back together, and together they were—all the time. It was young love at its very finest.

While John was focused on his gridiron future, Pat was quite busy at home. She was working at Sheridan Printing; she had started there in high school and did so well that she became an important part of the company. She was one of the main people with whom customers interacted, and therefore she became the face of the company to new customers and visitors. She started as a receptionist and eventually worked her way up to secretary to the vice president of sales.

At the same time, Pat was always helping her mother with her three young siblings: Susan, Richard and Mary Jane. When she was out with John for afternoon activities, she often took the kids with her. John didn't mind, and the children were always well-behaved.

One day John, Pat and her siblings visited their close friends Bob and Jul Mantoni. They spontaneously decided to go fishing at the Delaware River that bordered the town. It was not unusual for these spur-of-the-moment ideas to propel them into action. On this day, they decided to bring some steaks and build a fire for a cookout. At one point, John, wearing a pair of moccasins, stepped into an area of quicksand-like material without seeing it. He sank down to his thighs and couldn't move. Bob, Pat and the kids were laughing hysterically. If it had not been for Jul finding a strong branch and handing it to him, he would not have been able to get out. When he finally did manage to emerge, his shoes were not on his feet. Bob and Pat could not stop laughing. John was livid at all of them. The story stuck with each of them over the years that followed, and every time it came up, they all laughed.

The summer of '62 was a special one, and John was in the best shape of his life. He had worked out hard and was ready for the new challenge at Colgate. But then bad luck struck. Pat and John went to a picnic at his uncle's house, and a touch football game ensued. John joined in, but unfortunately he stepped in a hole while he was running and tore his hamstring muscle. It hemorrhaged and he was black and blue from his butt to his ankle. He was examined by a doctor, put on crutches, and arrived at Colgate injured and unable to play for several weeks. Again, he became the second-string quarterback.

Eventually, John worked his way to the starting position against the freshman team of Syracuse. He did well and completed numerous passes, but in the process of being tackled, he tore the ligaments in his ankle. John's freshman year of football was riddled with injuries that kept him from showing his coaches his true potential as a quarterback.

His parents, Rose and Jake, had become very fond of Pat and took her to games to see him play. Pat was gracious enough to put her hurt behind her, and the three of them, and sometimes John's brother Jim, attended games together. Somewhere along the way in John's gridiron career, Pat became the ultimate football fan. She loved the Dallas Cowboys and despised the Oakland Raiders. She eventually proved to love the game more than John, tuning in every Monday and Thursday night and on Sundays.

During his freshman year, many fraternities were courting John. A few of his friends, however, didn't have as many suitors. So he made a plan with them: they would only go to the fraternity house that would take them all. They would work hard to make that fraternity the best on campus. All agreed, and eventually they joined Kappa Delta Rho.

Colgate University is located in a remote town in New York named Hamilton. The trip from Phillipsburg to Hamilton was always fraught with unexpected and sometimes dangerous events. The highways were in reasonably good condition until you reached Binghamton, New York. Then the divided highway ended and Route 12 began. It was a two-lane road through rural countryside with herds of deer that often ran parallel to your car. Cattle sometimes wandered onto the road. Farm vehicles would occasionally pull out in front of you doing 15 miles per hour, enticing you to pass on a very dangerous and circuitous road. And then there was the snow that could engulf your car at any time. At Colgate, there was often snow from October to April or May. In the midst of winter, the snow would be piled 5 feet high on each side of the road. It was also very cold. It was not uncommon for the wind chill factor to make it feel like 20 degrees below zero.

At the time, Colgate had an all-male student body. There were three party weekends a year—Homecoming in the fall and parties in the winter and spring. Pat attended most of the parties. She took a bus the first time, but it took forever to get to Syracuse and then to Hamilton. On the return trip she missed a connection and had to stay overnight at the Port Authority Bus Terminal in New York City. Luckily, she found an older woman to be with during the night among the unsavory characters that inhabited the terminal. One other time she flew into Utica, New York, but it was also difficult for her to get to Hamilton from there, or for John to get her. After those attempts at public transportation, Pat resorted to driving. She would often take other girls with her who were going to the fraternity party.

All the guys tried to find rides for their girlfriends, so there was no shortage of potential passengers. Once in a snowstorm on Route 81, it began to snow so hard that only one lane was open. At one point, Pat's car did a 360-degree spin, and the girls were screaming in fear. Pat told them to shut up because it was difficult enough to navigate the road without a bunch of screaming passengers. When she finally arrived at Colgate, John, who had been worried sick about her driving in the awful weather, ran out to greet her. She said, "Don't touch me." She was so emotionally stressed from the drive and the screaming girls that she needed some downtime. While initially upset with her, John understood her emotional state once she relayed the story of the trip. She said she would never again take more than one or two girls with her.

Party weekends at Colgate were renowned. There were bands playing at all the frat houses, with flowing beer and dancing and partying into the wee hours of the morning.

Soon came Homecoming weekend in John's sophomore year. A friend and fraternity brother of John's had asked if Pat would bring his girlfriend. Pat agreed, and the two girls arrived on Thursday night. The two guys got to see their girls that night. On Friday night, however, both guys were to sleep at the field house with their football teammates. The coaches wanted to be sure they were ready for the game and not out late partying. John would risk anything to see Pat. The two guys decided it was unlikely they would get into the game on Saturday, so they developed a daring plan to sneak out of the field house and go party with the girls.

They chose bunks closest to a door that was at the very end of the room. When the lights were out and they were pretty sure all were asleep, they stuffed pillows under their blankets to give the appearance that they were sleeping. They quietly headed for the door, and as they exited they put a twig between the door and the doorframe. And away they went. They reached the fraternity and found their girlfriends doing tequila shots with lime and salt. The older fraternity brothers were teaching the young, pretty girls how to do it. John and his friend separated, each going off with his own girlfriend, and agreed to get back together at 2 a.m. to sneak back into the field house.

Pat and John went to a remote area by a cemetery, parked the station wagon and put the seats down. They talked and held each other for hours before going back to the party at the fraternity. John finally said that he had to get back to meet his friend.

At the appointed hour, after seeing the girls to the rooming house where they were staying, the two guys walked quietly across the field toward the field house. Suddenly, a dog appeared and began barking at them. It took a bit of doing, but they were finally able to scare the dog away. They were sure the dog was going to expose their caper. They managed to sneak back inside, grateful that the twig was still holding the door slightly ajar. They noiselessly closed the door and climbed back into bed. Their risky scheme had been a success, and both chalked it up to some very good luck—which was about to end.

CHAPTER 6

A Series of Unfortunate Events

JOHN WORKED HIS WAY TO A STARTING POSITION by the end of his sophomore year. He played half of the Yale game and was scheduled to be the starting quarterback for the last game of the 1963 season against Brown University on November 23. The Colgate bus arrived in Providence, Rhode Island around midday on Friday, November 22. Someone boarded the bus and informed the coaches and the team that President John Kennedy had been shot and had died. You could've heard a pin drop on the bus. The game was canceled, as there were more important matters than football to be addressed. It was a strange and somber time, and the fraternity brothers, like most of the nation, were glued to the TV. There were theories of conspiracies, foreign government involvement and even CIA involvement in the assassination of a very popular young president.

As the year progressed, John was selected to go to a quarterback camp in Oxford, Maine, run by a former All-Pro quarterback of the New York Giants, Benny Friedman. Five quarterbacks from around the country had been invited to the camp. The young men worked as camp counselors during the day, and in the middle of the day Benny would work with them. He taught the young men the mechanics of throwing the football, protecting themselves when they hit the ground, offensive strategies, and some very good advice about knowing which players were ready for the game. Benny invited newspapers and TV stations from the Boston area to observe the practice sessions and to take some videos of the guys waterskiing with a football under one arm.

During this period, Pat wrote John an unforgettable letter. In it she said, "I miss my 180 pounds of twisted steel and sex appeal." The letter made quite an impression on her beau.

When the summer ended, John returned to Colgate for preseason practice in his junior year. Benny had given the coaches his endorsement of John. One day the coaches had everyone tackling a dummy, which was mounted on a sled (with a coach standing on it). John was the last person to hit the dummy before going to passing drills. When he went to throw his first pass, he felt excruciating pain in his right shoulder. Tackling the dummy had separated his shoulder. His throwing arm was finished. So were his visions of becoming a starting quarterback for the next two years. He was absolutely devastated that his football career, in which he had hoped to accomplish so much, was suddenly over.

As Tom Parnell had promised Rose and Jake, John kept his scholarship. But he didn't feel right about just walking away from the team. He asked the head coach how he could help. It was decided that he would assist in coaching the freshmen backfield for his last two seasons.

As John and his friends were progressing to their junior year, it was time for them to take over leadership of the fraternity house. At the time, there were some fraternity brothers who were getting drunk on the weekends and then punching out windows and breaking furniture. Three of them were responsible for considerable damage to the house. John ran for president, saying he would put a stop to the outrageous behavior. He won by one vote. His roommate, Bob Brown, became the kitchen steward. John's freshman roommate, John Delvecchio, became the house manager. The plan from freshman year was working. They were now in position to put their plan into action.

John had met the treasurer of Colgate, John Falcone, on a number of occasions. One day he made an appointment with Falcone and presented a plan to renovate the fraternity house. John told him of the plan to make KDR the best house on campus by senior year. Over the next few months, Falcone worked with John and arranged the financing for the renovation, which was to take place over the summer months. In the meantime, the new fraternity officers and the management team worked on streamlining social programs, food menus and maintenance programs. There were many contentious interactions between the three offenders and John. Face-to-face confrontations nearly led to blows several times.

John was a waiter at the fraternity to pay for his board. One night after dinner, there was a fraternity house meeting in the dining room. The seniors wanted to use the house for graduation parties. John told them they had shown themselves to be irresponsible and had caused damage to the house. Jeff, a 6-foot-4-inch 240-pound troublemaker, was livid, but John didn't care. As John was walking past Jeff toward the kitchen, he "accidentally" moved a chair under a table, and it hit Jeff's leg.

In a loud voice, Jeff demanded an apology. The dining room became very quiet. John walked directly up to Jeff and told him to get up. John was ready for a fight. This guy had caused so much trouble for the fraternity, and John thought this would be the ultimate confrontation. Jeff turned red as though the top of his head might blow off. He looked at John with a long glaring stare, and then he looked away. John paused and then eventually moved away from him. The fraternity house would be locked up until renovations began, despite Jeff's protests.

Incredibly, Jeff and his cohorts broke into the house and created more damage. John immediately went to see Dean Griffin, the dean of students, and explained what was happening. Griffin said to John, "I want you to take a pad and pen and walk around the house recording every item that has been broken, cracked, destroyed or harmed in some manner. It doesn't have to be damage done in the past few days. After you do that, place a dollar figure on the damage. I will contact their parents and tell them their sons will not graduate unless restitution is made to you as president of the house, and I am notified by you that you have received the money." John thanked the dean and headed to KDR.

As John went around the house making his notes, the troublemakers asked what he was doing. He calmly said he was making a list of all the damage they had caused. They asked what he was going to do about it. He relayed what Griffin had told him. The kids weren't happy, but their parents were contacted, and the money was paid. John left Colgate after securing the fraternity house and was quite sure there would be no more damage done.

Over the summer months, John made several trips to Colgate to meet with Falcone and to review the progress of the renovations. New furniture was purchased for the common areas, and all was moving along nicely and on schedule. When September rolled around and the students returned to Colgate, the KDR members found that a spectacular metamorphosis had occurred. Their fraternity had been transformed into a model facility. Everything was new and improved. Rooms were renovated, and some single residence rooms were transformed into suites. The living room, dining room, downstairs bar and party room were all new.

Bob Brown was the rushing chairman. He and the team did a great job of attracting impressive young men to the fraternity. A cast of new pledges brought with it a fresh and upbeat culture. The bad apples were gone, and KDR became an exemplary fraternity.

By this time, Pat had joined John on many party weekends and was known by all the fraternity members. She was beautiful, and she was engaging and personable with all the brothers. Once again, the young couple was on a comfortable path together.

Unfortunately, trouble would enter the picture again, this time in the winter of John's senior year. John was riding in a car with fraternity brothers Pete McGinnis, Larry Carrol and Steve Hepburn. Seat belts did not exist at this time. Pete was driving and Steve was sitting behind him. John was in the front passenger seat, and Larry was behind him. Pete had an Oldsmobile Cutlass convertible. It was a cold December day, and final exams were in progress. The four students were going to Giordano's restaurant for something to eat and to take a break from studying. As they passed the Colgate field house and hospital on the rural, two-lane Route 12, a tractor-trailer was coming in the opposite direction. The lights of the massive truck temporarily blinded Pete's vision at exactly the wrong moment.

Incredibly, a drunk driver had parked a large truck on the road, and it extended four feet into the lane where the students were driving. In a flash, John saw it and screamed. He put his arm up to protect himself from the collision, but it was too late. The car smashed into the parked truck. The force caused the front windshield to shatter and collapse onto John. He felt a cut on his head, so he took out a handkerchief and put it to his head near his eye. It came back bright red, for he was badly injured. His temporal artery was cut, and his right ankle was broken from bracing himself for the collision.

As he turned to look in the back seat, John saw Larry keeled over on his side, bleeding profusely. John went into shock. Pete had lost a tooth and Steve had a slight scratch from the flying glass; both were very lucky. They were immediately transported to the Colgate Hospital. John and Larry were incredibly fortunate that the accident hadn't happened on the even more rural road to Giordano's. John was sedated on the operating table, but he was aware of being stitched up by the doctor. He had no idea where Larry was or if he had survived. Just then Dean Griffin came into the emergency room and asked, "Which one is Gammino?" Obviously, this scared the heck out of John. If the dean had to ask that, John must've been in very bad shape. He knew he couldn't die.

He kept saying to the doctor, "Don't let me die; I want to marry Pat. Don't let me die; I want to marry Pat." He said it over and over as he was being stitched with 45 sutures in his forehead and around his eye. A cast was put on his right ankle after the bone was reset. When he was transported from the emergency room to a patient room, Larry was in the bed across from him. He and Larry could see each other, but not themselves. They were put on Demerol. Larry told John that the right side of his head was very swollen. John's eye was closed, and the stitches ran in a vertical line from the top of his forehead to just above the eye. There were even stitches in his eyelid. John told Larry, "I can't tell what's under the bandages on your face. It looks like there are cuts on your face below and above the bandages." (It turned out there were 90 stitches in his face.) They were both so drugged that they handled the information with ease.

The next morning some members of the football team came to see them. These were tough guys. They took one look at their friends, said how sorry they were for what had happened, and then left in a hurry. John and Larry looked like they had come out of a horror show. Around noon, Rose, Jake and Pat came to visit. Rose fainted after taking one look at her son, and they had to take her to another room to revive her. Pat handled the ugly, stitched face and broken ankle like a trooper, as did Jake.

The doctor came into the room while Jake and Pat were there. When he found out her name was Pat, he told her what John had repeatedly said during his surgery. Pat was touched by the news, but also sad to see him in that condition. However, the doctor said John would make a complete recovery. John would later say that his priorities became very clear when he thought he was going to die. He realized that he and Pat should not have to wait any longer to declare their love forever.

Somehow, Larry and John managed to laugh at their situation. They were unable to see their own faces, but based on the reactions of all the people who came to visit them, they figured they must be a mess. Pain medication made them giddy in spite of their situation. Reality did sink in a few days later when they were given mirrors so they could look at themselves. It was both a somber and a shocking moment for each young man, and it brought home the reality of how grateful they were to have survived such a harrowing accident.

Shortly thereafter, John returned home for Christmas break. He was on crutches, and the stitches had been removed from his face. His face was still swollen, but his eye was now open, and he could see with both eyes. John made good on his hospital pledge and asked Pat to marry him one night. He had grand plans of asking her during a romantic dinner, but the restaurant was closed, so he asked her in the car. Even though the setting wasn't what he had planned, both were ecstatic, and they set their wedding date for June 4, 1966, which was the Saturday after he graduated from Colgate. Before the big day, however, John had to prepare himself in other big ways.

CHAPTER 7

Preparing for the Real World

AS A PSYCHOLOGY MAJOR, JOHN HAD TO FACE
the possibility of going on to graduate school or finding
a job in some other field. It was an uncertain time for him. He
had many discussions with his friends at Colgate; however,
none of them understood the business world. There were
no role models in most of their families. John decided to
take some initiative, and he asked the placement director at
Colgate if he would come to a fraternity house meeting to
discuss opportunities for graduates in the business world.
The placement director agreed and explained to the fraternity members that his office had material on 300 companies
that would be coming to campus in the spring to interview
potential hires. Meeting attendees were advised to select
roughly six companies in which they had an interest and
then do research on the companies' management programs.
They were also advised to take one or two interviews with
companies they didn't care about, just to gain experience
with the whole process.

John spent considerable time at the placement office reviewing company literature, and then he had his first interview, with Exxon. The Exxon representative began by asking John just how he might make a contribution to the company. He stumbled through an answer. Then the rep asked, "What are your strengths?" John was in disbelief. *What are my strengths?* Again, his answer was not very solid. The next question was, "What are your weaknesses?" By this time, the interview was on its way to the trash can. John botched every answer, because he hadn't thought about these kinds of questions. He was embarrassed and wanted to get out of the interview as soon as he could. That was easy when the rep said, "I think you would agree that you are not a match for Exxon." John agreed, thanked him for his time and sped back to his room. He appreciated the placement director's wisdom about taking additional interviews to gain experience.

John made a promise to himself that he would never be so unprepared for an interview again. He crafted answers to the strengths and weaknesses questions. He developed a description of the management accomplishments he had demonstrated as president of the fraternity. He was good and ready for his interview with Connecticut General Insurance Company.

When the representative of Connecticut General asked John what he thought he could contribute to the company, John was ready. He moved into a discussion of his management experience at KDR. He spoke of planning, organizing, directing and controlling. He shared some accomplishments: stopping the destruction of the fraternity house, the planning and financing of the renovation, and the way he and his friends had acquired management positions so they could make the frat house the best on campus. He spoke of the multifaceted plan to improve the rushing process to bring in members with various backgrounds and capabilities. He mentioned that they had improved the cooking and the cleaning with new hires. He also mentioned a charitable endeavor: the fraternity had hosted poor children and their parents during the Christmas season so they could give the kids toys and a fun afternoon.

John knew by the reaction of the interviewer that he had made his points with clarity and confidence. He was now interviewing the interviewer about why he should join his company. Where might a guy like himself be in five years in terms of position and income? What benefits would be provided, etc.?

By the time John got to the New Jersey Bell interview, he was razor sharp. This was the company he wanted most, for two main reasons. First, Pat didn't want to move out of New Jersey, and this seemed like a nice fit. Second, the management program was a high-risk, high-reward challenge. If the new hire could demonstrate potential for the third level of management within the first year, he would be fast-tracked to that level in three to five years. If the new hire couldn't demonstrate that potential, he would be fired in the first year. Though it was a daunting scenario, John welcomed the challenge and the opportunity to move up quickly.

The interview with New Jersey Bell resulted in an invitation to visit the company's headquarters, which was in Newark. The company paid for a round-trip flight. John was introduced to various people and was given an overview of the company and its departments. Arrangements were made for him to be taken to Phillipsburg to meet Pat for lunch; the local business office manager and the HR representative would attend as well. After a lovely lunch and an attempt by the company representatives to woo Pat as an ally, John was taken back to Newark. He later learned that Pat was impressed that they would think enough of him to bring him all the way to Phillipsburg to meet her.

John went on to visits to Connecticut General, Sears, Scott Paper Company and others. Eventually, the offers began coming in, and the New Jersey Bell offer was among them. While New Jersey Bell did not offer the highest salary, John chose it for what he considered to be a bright future.

Several weeks before graduation, Pat and John learned that his first assignment would be in Elizabeth, New Jersey. He came home for a weekend and went apartment hunting with Pat. They settled on a new apartment complex called Exeter House. It was close to his first job location, and the rent was $127 per month. John's gross salary would be $550 per month.

John went back to Colgate and graduated in May of 1966. On June 4, one week after graduation, John and Pat were married at St. Philip and St. James Catholic Church in Phillipsburg. The wedding and honeymoon were a mix of joy, anticipation, and unexpected realities.

CHAPTER 8

At Long Last: The Wedding

PAT HAD BEEN WORKING AT SHERIDAN PRINTING, and she had saved enough money for a reception with 350 people at the Phillipsburg Elks Club. During his last semester, John ran the soda machine concession at the fraternity house, and he had saved as much as he could. He accumulated enough money to pay for flights to Bermuda, the hotel, and their honeymoon. The rest would have to come from wedding gifts. They would literally start their marriage with zero money.

On Thursday, June 2, a party was held at the Gamminos' house after the wedding rehearsal. His parents refinished the basement and installed a bar to prepare for the party. It was a time of celebration, and everyone had a great time.

On the morning of June 4, Pat had her hair done and took her father to be shaved by the barber. John had predicted to Bob and Larry, two of his groomsmen, that Pat would probably be late, as she often was in those days. On this day, however, he was wrong.

At precisely 11 a.m. on June 4, the chimes of the church rang out, the organ music began, and the procession of flower girls and bridesmaids was under way. Following them was the bride, who was escorted down the aisle by her father, Tony. The organ music gave John the chills, but in a good way. He was speechless when he saw the beautiful woman walking down the aisle toward him. Pat looked up at the handsome man she was about to join for life. They were ecstatic that this day had finally arrived. They were both 22 and had overcome so many difficult obstacles to get here.

Pat's father lifted her veil and kissed her on the cheek. His face was flushed with nervousness as he handed his precious daughter over to her husband-to-be. When Monsignor Kozak declared John and Pat man and wife, there was an outpouring of applause. John kissed Pat, and both were as happy as two little kids in a candy store. Their special love was obvious to all who attended.

The reception was a major celebration, but it went by like a blur for the newlyweds. They did enjoy the eight-piece orchestra, especially when it performed "More" by Brook Benton for their first dance. They made sure to visit each table to thank all the folks who had come.

At the end of the evening, Pat and John opened envelopes that were gifted to them and recorded what each guest had given so they could send thank-you notes when they returned from their honeymoon.

The couple settled in for the night at their motel near the airport. John was anxious to sleep with his bride. However, Pat began crying, and he was quite shocked. He asked what was wrong, and she said she missed her father. John was in disbelief. He thought, *We are 35 minutes from home on the first night of our marriage and she is crying that she misses her father?*

At long last, the happy couple was joined in matrimony on June 4, 1966.

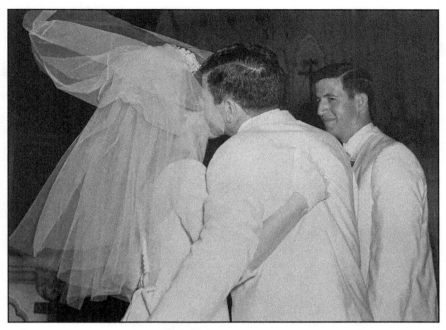

Pat's father lifted her veil and kissed her on the cheek before handing her to John.

It would not be the first time that expectations and reality were far apart. They hugged and kissed each other goodnight. Anything else would have to wait until they arrived in Bermuda.

In the morning, Pat apologized to John and said she didn't know what had come over her. She said she would make it up to him. John smiled, because of course he would be very eager for that to happen. When they arrived at the Eastern Airlines gate, John checked in with the gate attendant, who looked at the newlyweds and smiled. He had guessed they were on their honeymoon and decided to upgrade them to first class. John didn't know what that meant. He had only flown a few times, and it was always in coach.

The couple couldn't believe the lap of luxury into which they had landed. Spacious seats, amazing service and even

The couple had a fabulous time in Bermuda on their honeymoon.

free booze. They were pretty shocked that alcohol was served in the morning, but John gamely went along and ordered a screwdriver. Later, when he saw others accepting wine from the flight attendant, he did as well. Pat had Baileys and cream.

When they arrived in Bermuda, they had to go through customs, and they were nervous because this was the first time they'd had to face another government's authority. They had no trouble getting through, and they took a cab to the Hamilton Princess Hotel downtown, which was absolutely beautiful. The room was much nicer than John had expected.

The waiters at the hotel were all French and Italian and never missed an opportunity to flatter or flirt with the guests. When John and Pat arrived at dinner, the waiter pulled out the chair for Pat and, with a charming accent, told her how beautiful she looked. Pat loved that and everything else about the trip so far.

She whispered, "Good job, honey." That evening the newlyweds were wined and dined in a style to which they were definitely not accustomed.

In the morning, they decided to take the hotel van to Princess Beach. When they arrived, they discovered luscious pink sand. The water was crystal clear, and you could still see your feet when immersed chest deep. Pat and John were in paradise. He had chosen the right place for them to start their new life together. He wondered if it was a dream. Pat looked gorgeous. Her flowing brown hair and greenish-blue eyes complemented a beautiful body. She was a knockout. John was handsome and in great shape. He worked out a lot and kept his body firm and lean. Together they made a very striking couple.

Pat and John toast another trip to Bermuda.

The Gamminos loved Bermuda so much they returned 11 times.

At dinner they met Jackie and Steve, also newlyweds who were on their honeymoon. They agreed to meet in the morning for breakfast and then go for a ride on motorbikes.

The couples set off on the motorbikes the next morning. At one point Pat turned the handle of her bike too far, and the bike accelerated and shot her front wheel into the air. Her glasses went flying, but fortunately she was not hurt. John decided they would go back and get a two-seater. Pat was happy to sit behind John and hold onto him as they rode over the narrow, winding roads of Bermuda. The couples enjoyed some time together taking in the breathtaking scenery on the south shore, but Pat and John were anxious to explore more of the island, so they left after a few hours.

A week in the Bermuda sun and sea had turned them into suntanned beauties. Their honeymoon was coming to an end, and they were looking forward to beginning their new life together in New Jersey.

When they arrived at the airport, they were surprised to discover that their seats were in the back of the plane. The gate attendant explained that they had been given a complimentary upgrade for their trip *to* Bermuda. Although they understood, they were obviously disappointed to miss out on the first-class service. Perhaps it prepared them for some disappointments that awaited in their first apartment together and in John's new job.

CHAPTER 9

The New Job

WHEN THEY RETURNED FROM THEIR HONeymoon, Pat and John visited with their parents. Pat went immediately to her father's store to give him a hug and kiss. She was now a married woman about to embark on a new life that would take her away from her home.

After visiting her mom and John's parents, they headed for their first apartment in Elizabeth, New Jersey. John was to begin his career at New Jersey Bell the following week. They sat on boxes and folding chairs around an inexpensive card table until they had enough money to buy dining room furniture. John's Aunt Rose had provided money for them to buy a bedroom set and living room furniture. John and Pat revered his Aunt Rose. She had always filled Christmas and Easter holidays with toys, new clothes and other surprises for John and his brother. She loved Pat like the daughter she never had.

The apartment they had rented on their one-day search was brand new. They were happy with the space, but soon learned that they hadn't done enough due diligence. The small

TV that they bought at Sears was connected to the antenna on top of the apartment building. They didn't realize that the apartment was within the air traffic pattern for Newark Airport. Each time a plane would pass over, you couldn't hear the TV and the picture would jump from frame to frame, and black lines would slowly progress from the bottom to the top of the screen. Needless to say, it was annoying. In addition, there were loud trains directly behind the apartments that were hidden by a high fence, and late at night kids would drag race on the streets in front of the apartment. They mused to each other that they would be more careful next time when selecting a place to live.

On his first day of work, John reported to George Warner, the district manager of traffic engineering. George presided over the determination of what switching and other facilities were necessary to accommodate the growth in calls over the New Jersey Bell network. The job had its complexities, and John was very confused on day one. People spoke in terms that were foreign. They discussed "trunks, lines and offices." By the end of day one, he was speaking a new language.

George was a great boss and told John there was much to learn, and he spent several hours every Friday with John going over his reading assignments. George accelerated John's learning curve, and very quickly John was able to discuss the most complex matters involving switches and other facilities.

Because John and Pat's apartment was close to his office, John would often come home for lunch. They were still in the honeymoon phase of their marriage, and John wanted to be sure that Pat, who was a homemaker, did not feel alone all day long.

Meanwhile, George was so impressed with John's speed of learning that he arranged for John to move on in the business and be challenged with more responsibility.

After just three months on the job, John was transferred to the Atlantic City District and became responsible for managing three operator locations with 400 people. Pat and John were delighted. They were able to get a larger, less expensive apartment in Margate that was close to the beach. Their two-bedroom apartment had a deck and its own parking space. Shortly after they moved in, the couple was thrilled to learn that Pat was pregnant. They were ecstatic about having the first child from their marriage.

John's new boss in Atlantic City was Tom Taylor. John knew that he would either be fast-tracked for promotion to district manager or fired within the first year. The stakes were high; Tom had fired the last five college hires, including one from Colgate University.

After his first day of work in the new location, John called Pat and said that the guys at work were taking John's predecessor, Charlie, out to dinner. After dinner, they took Charlie out on the town, and John went along as the newbie, not knowing where they were going. He had never been to strip clubs and was pretty astonished at the activities that took place within them; however, he had to play it cool, as he had just met his boss and his colleagues.

John didn't return home until 4 a.m. As he started to put the key in the lock, the door swung open and his new bride demanded to know where he had been. He told her he didn't know they would be out that long and that they had been bar hopping. He thought it would be wise to leave out the bit about the strip clubs. That night Pat and John slept in separate beds.

Of course, John's decision came back to haunt him a few months later. One night, after having dinner with their new neighbors, Bob and Dolly Smith, Bob suggested they go to a strip club. Dolly said, "John, you've already been to the Hialeah Club, haven't you?" John ignored her, but Pat didn't miss a beat. She said angrily, "Finally I find out where you were that night." John promised Pat that he would not keep secrets like that from her anymore. He said he had been embarrassed to admit that's where they were that night.

Late nights became the norm when the team had to work on provisional estimates. They had to predict the number of calls and operators they would need for 18 months into the future. This happened each quarter. On those evenings, the wives just took it for granted that their husbands would be home late.

John was challenged. He asked a lot of questions about his predecessor's performance and approach. He determined that the best approach was the one he always preferred—humility. Each of the operator locations was managed by a chief operator. John had three chief operators reporting to him. He met with each one and told them he would be appreciative if they would help him learn the business and keep him from making major mistakes. John was 22 years of age. Each of the chief operators was old enough to be his mother, and in one case his grandmother. John made a point of treating them with courtesy and respect. Each of them protected him as a mother would protect her son. John was a fast learner. After six months, he evolved naturally into the boss, and he engendered the respect of the chief operators and their staffs.

With things falling into place at work, life at home was decidedly less orderly—more characterized by unforgettable adventures and antics.

CHAPTER 10

Margate Madness

WHILE JOHN WAS AT WORK, PAT MET SOME older neighborhood men who became enamored with the pregnant young woman who had just moved into the neighborhood. Morris and Griff were two Jewish men who were kind to her and looked after her as she went to the beach each day. Pat didn't have a lot of maternity clothes, and the couple was basically broke. Pat wore a pair of John's shorts backwards and used a rope to tie them around her bulging waist. She thought this was hilarious, and so did her two new friends.

There was another friend who would join Pat each day at the beach. Her name was Patti Lane, and Patti's husband, Fred, was in the same program as John but worked for a different district manager. The four young people were together all the time. They enjoyed dinner and dancing on weekends and during the week they would visit each other's apartments. It turned out that there was a lot to do in Atlantic City and the surrounding areas of Margate, Ocean City and Somers Point.

Throughout the pregnancy Pat was very radiant. One day she called John and said her water broke while she was shopping. John was both excited and nervous, and asked if she had labor pains. She said they were just beginning, and she was going to the obstetrician. John told Fred, and they decided to have a labor party to time her pains. The pains were 10 minutes apart for some time. Patti, Fred and John were having drinks and saluting Pat and the baby.

Each of them thought the birth would be imminent, but it wasn't. Patti and Fred went home around midnight. John was tired and tense. He dozed off to sleep at 12:30. At 3:30 Pat woke him to say she thought she was ready to deliver. John jumped up and asked about the timing of the labor pains and if she had called the doctor. He was a nervous mess, but Pat was very calm. Both knew the plan was for the baby to be delivered at the nearby Shore Memorial Hospital in Somers Point.

John had scoped out the time it would take to drive from the apartment to the hospital, and he knew he could get there in 10 minutes or less. When Pat got off the phone, she told John that the doctor was at Atlantic City Hospital and that she would have to be taken there. John, who was usually good at handling stressful situations, became visibly upset. He said tersely, "Atlantic City?"

Pat confirmed: "Yes, Atlantic City."

All the way there, they hit traffic light after traffic light, and the stress level was increasing for both of them. When they finally arrived, the hospital door was locked, and a sign told them to use the emergency entrance. That entrance was on the other side of the hospital, which meant the possibility of four traffic lights, since the hospital took up a full city block.

John asked Pat if she would be able to walk to it, which would be faster than driving. She said she could. Unfortunately, neither counted on the need to go over hedges and other obstacles. The stress had reached a fever pitch. When they finally got to the emergency entrance, there was no one there except a guy sleeping on a couch. As it turned out, he was the night manager of the emergency room. He asked John for his insurance card and began the admittance process. Pat was getting upset and said she needed a waste can because she was going to be sick. The man gave her a waste can and continued asking questions. John said firmly, "You get her upstairs to the maternity ward, and I will answer your questions." The manager did not respond, so Pat took matters into her own hands. She screamed at him that if he didn't get her upstairs quickly, she was going to have the baby right there. That motivated the guy to take her upstairs.

When the manager returned, he and John finished the check-in process. John made it to the maternity floor, and Pat had the baby less than five minutes later. At that time, fathers were not allowed in the delivery room. When the doctor came out to tell John that Pat had a little girl and that both the baby and Pat were fine, John let out a sigh of relief. He asked when he could see them, and he was told the nurse would come to get him in a few minutes.

Pat was in pain from the delivery, but she still had the glow of a mother who had just created a miracle. John was so proud of her and himself for creating this beautiful baby with a full head of hair. Her name was Maureen. She was born at 4:20 a.m. Pat and John were both exhausted. The nurse told John he should go home and get some sleep. After kissing Pat and Maureen, John drove back to the apartment and called both sets of grandparents, who of course were elated by the news.

After getting a few hours of sleep, John went back to the hospital. Pat looked refreshed from the rest, and they hugged each other with a new, gentle warmth and a new dimension of love. They were proud parents. Pat came home from the hospital with Maureen, and a new phase of their life began. Pat and John took Maureen with them wherever they went.

There were four apartments in the building where Pat and John lived. Each had a parking space in front of the building. When John came home from work one day, someone was parked in his spot. He was peeved and couldn't find anywhere else to park. It was as if there had been an invasion and every street was full of parked cars. He finally found a parking place and walked to his apartment. He wrote a note and placed it on the windshield of the car in his spot. The note said that the car was parked illegally, and if it wasn't moved by later that evening, he would have it towed. It was then that Pat and John learned that the quiet community they'd moved into in September was a favorite spot for college kids in the summer. It was a seasonal town, and in the summer the population swelled to overflowing.

The building next to Pat and John's was no more than 3 feet away on the bedroom side of their apartment. There was no air conditioning, so the windows were open. The college kids rented the building by floor, girls on the first floor and guys on the second. But it didn't take long for them to mingle. Pat and John were entertained by some of their antics.

After six weeks, Pat went back to the doctor and was to be cleared for marital activity for the first time since Maureen was born. In those days there was a joke that the guys told about just such an event. It started with a question: How soon after your wife has a baby do you return to having sex? After a pause the answer was: That depends on if she has a private or a semiprivate room. This joke would always get a roar from the guys. When Pat received her clearance from the doctor, John was delighted but made the mistake of mentioning it to Fred and his boss. This was to be his night. However, at about 7 p.m., there was a knock at the door. When John opened it,

there stood his work associates and their wives with cases of
beer and wine. He asked what the occasion was. They said there
was no way John was going to have sex that night, because
they were there to get him drunk. They accomplished their
mission, and sex had to wait until another night.

Shortly thereafter, John's parents came to visit Margate for
the first time. Rose and Jake were in one bedroom, and John
and Pat were in the other. The walls were paper thin, and you
could hear most things easily. Pat was in an amorous mood. She
snuggled up to John in bed and began playfully touching and
caressing him. He found her playfulness amusing and welcome.
However, she decided to go beyond that and take it to a new
level. John whispered for her to stop. He said, "They're going
to hear us." Pat didn't care. This was her residence and she
was not intimidated by John's parents. John was embarrassed
but finally decided that married people could do anything they
wanted. The next morning there was no sign of discomfort in
John's parents, and he was happy about that.

Kathleen Vayda, Pat's cousin and maid of honor, also came
for a visit. Her husband, Bob, was a fireman, and there was a
convention of firefighters in Atlantic City. Kathleen and Bob
said they'd heard there were strip clubs in Atlantic City, and
they would like to go. Pat knew that John had been to several,
and she said she would like to go as well.

When the couples entered the Hialeah Club, they were
escorted to a table close to the stage. John had told Pat about
a dancer he had seen there who went by the name of Tammy
True. He said he couldn't take his eyes off of her, she was so
beautiful. When Tammy came out, John was anxious to see
the reactions of the others at the table. As she stripped off her
clothing, Tammy had her eyes riveted on Pat. It was as if she
was in love with her. John was disappointed, but Pat thought
it was funny, as did Kathleen and Bob.

There were two little people who were part of the act. They would look at Pat, stick their tongues out, move them back and forth, and mouth the words "I love you." Pat was disgusted by this portion of the show, but John thought it was hilarious. They would both come to laugh about this experience years later.

Another laugh came when Pat's parents came to visit Margate. Her mother had given her a pet parakeet for Maureen. Maureen was very fond of the parakeet, and Pat had taught the little bird to repeat certain words. One day, Pat had the sliding glass door open to let fresh air into the apartment. As she was cleaning the bird's cage, it flew out the window and was nowhere to be seen. Pat went out to buy a parakeet that looked like the one her mother had given her. She went to many pet stores, and the bird she settled on was a close match. However, it wasn't close enough for Ina, who asked Pat if it was the same parakeet that she had given her. Pat kept a straight face for a moment and then broke into hysterics. She told her mother the story and couldn't stop laughing. She was busted.

Jake also came to visit the young couple when he was in town for a convention. At the time, Maureen was a little tyke, but she was very conversant. One night at dinner, she told him a story: "You know what, PopPop? My mommy and my daddy were in the bathtub, and my daddy was pretending to be a seal."

Jake pretended he didn't hear her. Maureen wouldn't be denied, so she said it again. Jake's eyes rose from his downward glance as all three of them burst out laughing.

John later explained that they had been late for a dinner date, and he'd jumped into the tub with Pat. While he was fooling around with Pat, Maureen came into the room, and he began to splash the water. He told her he was pretending to be a seal. He knew it was a stupid thing to say, but he was shocked that she had caught them in the tub together. This event had taken place three weeks earlier and Maureen hadn't said a word about it until Jake arrived. The laughter and lightness of the situation would soon give way to a more serious era for the family that would be filled with personal and professional challenges.

CHAPTER II

Additional Challenges

PAT AND JOHN HAD BEEN MARRIED FOR JUST under two years when they received news that Pat's father, Tony, had died of a heart attack. He was just 54 years old, and it was absolutely devastating for his family. John had answered the phone to hear Pat's younger sister, Susan, crying hysterically and saying her father had died. Pat and John couldn't believe it; Tony was so young. They packed the car the next morning and drove from Margate to Phillipsburg. It was a heart-wrenching time for Pat. She was very close to her parents, and the loss of her father at such a young age was shocking.

Ina, Pat's mother, would now be a widowed mom with three children to raise by herself. She got a job at a meat market nearby and also baked and did sewing gigs on the side for money to manage her family's needs. Pat and John made frequent trips to visit Ina and the three younger kids. They tried as best they could to be supportive and helpful to Ina at that terrible time.

Occasionally, they would bring one or more of the kids back to Margate with them for a week. On one such occasion they

Pat's parents, Tony and Ina Morello (seated), enjoy a wedding with Tony's sister Mary and cousin Sal.

brought Mary Jane with them. On the ride to Margate, Mary Jane, who was 6 years old at the time, began to talk about Pat, whom she called Patsy. She said, "Patsy does everything. Patsy does the wash. Patsy does the ironing. Patsy does the cooking. Patsy does the dishes. Patsy does the cleaning." Then she said to John, "You work for the telephone company. All you do is sit with your feet on the desk and talk on the phone." Apparently, this was the vision the youngster had of what it meant to work at the phone company. Pat and John busted out laughing. John told Pat he thought she laughed a little too much, but this only caused the two of them to laugh even harder.

Pat and John loved their life in Margate. It was a great place to live and there were many benefits with the ocean and the social activities for young people surrounding them. When all the college kids left in September, it was even better. The cacophony of summer — bands playing in backyards, beer parties and nightclubs — was striking when compared to the serenity of the fall and winter months. In the off season, they had the beach and the clubs to themselves and a manageable group of other year-round residents.

One Saturday morning, John's boss, Tom Taylor, called and told him to pack a bag and go to Glassboro State College, where President Lyndon Johnson and Soviet Union Premier Alexei Kosygin were going to have a Summit conference. Tom asked John to establish an "outgoing message center for the press." John drove to Glassboro wondering *What exactly is that?* When he arrived at the college, he met with some of the other New Jersey Bell advance team members and asked every question he could. *How many press people are expected? From what countries? What equipment do we have to serve them? What is the schedule of events? Where can we locate the message center?* And so on.

John quickly learned that the three major TV networks, NBC, ABC and CBS, would be covering the speeches by the two leaders. When John asked what equipment was available to serve the press, he was appalled to learn that there was no mobile telephone platform to bring to the site. In one of his previous jobs, John had been responsible for maintenance of the POTUS board, which was the communications switchboard for the president of the United States. The Army Signal Corps brought the POTUS board to locations where the president would be. John thought there must be something similar to serve events like this. He was wrong; he learned that only Stone Age tools were available. He had to bring in live operators and set up sawhorses and plywood tables so that the operators could make out toll tickets for each call made by the press (for billing purposes). All told, there were 15 operators, 15 telephones and a few payphones on the other side of the campus to serve 1,200 international press people who all wanted to communicate to their offices at the same time. It was going to be utter mayhem.

The security was extremely tight for the event. The FBI, the Secret Service, state police officers and other undercover reps from both governments were all over the place, and they were searching everyone and checking credentials carefully. Police officers were on rooftops with rifles and machine guns. Crowds had gathered at every entrance and exit of the college. The helicopters arrived in caravan style, and you couldn't tell who was in which copter. The tension in the air was very high.

John probably hadn't had a busier day in his life, but he realized that the operators had to be hungry after having been on duty for eight hours with no food. He called for refreshments to be delivered. An hour later, a state police car with sirens blaring and lights flashing escorted a New Jersey Bell vehicle to the site. Two cases of soda and several boxes of submarine sandwiches were delivered to the team.

Everyone was in awe of what had just happened, but John thought the security teams would be livid about it. Not so! They were all very hungry too, as they hadn't eaten the entire time either. So John was able to take care of his team and some of the security detail that was guarding the gate nearest him. He soon became a popular figure with the police, but John began to worry that the soda bottles could be weaponized. Fortunately, they were not.

Miraculously, John and the operators were able to keep up with most of the press needs. Afterward, they all complimented John on how he had handled the assignment. He was glad of the praise but also happy to return to Margate and the simple life that he and Pat were living there.

However, their life in Margate was short-lived. After two years, John was transferred to Newark and became responsible for telecommunications services in the city. His new territory covered the business district, the seaport and airport, and residential areas that had recently been blighted by burned buildings and riots.

Pat and John needed to find an apartment that they could afford, but it was a daunting task. One of their high school friends lived in a town called Hillside and knew of a first-floor apartment available in a two-family home. It needed a lot of work, but it was in the couple's affordability range. John and some family members went to work painting and carpeting the entire apartment, thereby transforming it into a very nice living space.

In addition to managing telecommunications services, John was to oversee the installation of a new communications system that would be installed in the Newark Airport Tower. The system was to be interconnected to Kennedy and LaGuardia airports, which meant that if a flight pattern conflict arose, the controllers could communicate with one another instantly. It was a daunting assignment. John could not understand how, with just two years in the business and with a psychology background, he could be given such an important and technical job.

He decided to ask around and find out who was the most technically competent foreman. The name that came up often was Hal Squire. John met with Hal and made him an offer. He told Hal that he would release him from his current responsibilities and put him in charge of the technical part of the project. John told Hal he would get him everything he needed to get the job done and that Hal was to make sure the installation was flawless. Hal accepted, and the two went on together to manage the project. John had to make presentations to executives on the plans and the progress of the project, which he handled well.

On the night of cutover from the old system to the new system, there was no turning back. The new system simply had to work. The cutover was scheduled for 2 a.m. At the appointed time, the old system's cables were cut. The massive new system worked, and only two cable pairs had to be fixed. They were fixed in a few minutes. It was a huge success.

After spending 10 months in Newark, John was transferred back to Atlantic City, this time with a promotion to district manager. He had accomplished in two and a half years what was supposed to take three to five years. But John wasn't the only one making strides. Back at home, Pat was making impressive moves, too.

CHAPTER 12

Adaptable Pat

JOHN AND PAT MOVED QUITE A LOT DURING THE first five years of his career with New Jersey Bell. As John climbed the corporate ladder, Pat was busy caring for Maureen, decorating houses, finding new doctors, and re-establishing professional relationships.

During John's second tour in Atlantic City, the couple was thrilled when Melissa was born. This time John wasn't taking any chances. When Pat's pains were 10 minutes apart, he took her to the hospital, so she was there nine hours before she gave birth. There was no climbing over hedges or bushes this time. At one point, the doctor told him to go home and get some sleep and that he would call when the birth was imminent. When the doctor called, he said that Pat had had a baby girl. John was in a deep sleep and forgot to ask her height and weight. A call to Ina made him realize he had better get to the hospital and get more details. He did, and he relayed them to Ina and to Rose and Jake. All were delighted. Baby Melissa was beautiful. Pat and John were again very proud.

At the time, they lived in Absecon, New Jersey. They had to borrow money from Pat's mother's insurance policy for a down payment on a new home they were buying. It was a beautiful three-bedroom, split-level house with two and a half baths. They bought it before it was finished and therefore had the opportunity to choose colors, carpeting and cabinets. When it was completed, Pat and John were delighted with their first home. They were 26 years old. John had grown up in a four-room Cape Cod home with one bathroom. It wasn't until he was getting married that his parents remodeled the basement to create more living space. Before then, the basement was for the coal bin, the furnace, and storage of bicycles and other personal effects. Pat had lived in half of a double house with two stories and an attic. It was an older home and although it provided more living space than John's childhood home, its infrastructure was antiquated. Pat and John's new home was equipped with the latest features, and their families were very proud of how far they had come in such a short time.

The neighborhood in Absecon was all new. Homes were being built on their street and all around them. There were lots of young couples with preschool children, and Pat loved it. As usual, she made friends quickly and adapted well. John and Pat were extremely happy with their new home and their new neighbors. John had many friends at the company, and that allowed for many social activities. It was a lifestyle that allowed them to attend the Miss America Pageant at Convention Hall in Atlantic City, dine at a host of nice restaurants, walk on the famous Boardwalk, and enjoy the Somers Point and Ocean City social life as well.

As had been the case before, just when they had settled in and become involved in the community, John got transferred again, this time to headquarters in Newark. Again, neither Pat nor John was happy with the news. They went on house hunting trips in the northern New Jersey area and couldn't find a house they could afford that was in a decent neighborhood with good schools for the kids and a reasonable commute for John.

Finally, John heard of a home in Lincroft that was available through his company, which had bought it from a Bell Labs employee. Pat and John learned that you could sell your house to the company but could generally do better by listing it with a real estate agent. However, when you *bought* a house through the company, you got a price advantage. Pat and John looked at the four-bedroom, three-bathroom house on a cul-de-sac with a three-quarter-acre lot. The price was $39,900. They didn't know how they could possibly afford the $10,000 down payment. They had paid $22,600 for the new Absecon home two years before. Even with a $10,000 down payment, the mortgage for Lincroft would be nearly double what they were paying in Absecon.

John secured an agent and began the process of listing the Absecon house. He was going to list it at $34,600. The neighbors thought he was crazy and would not get that amount. Before the house was officially listed, a dentist who was looking to move into the neighborhood contacted the real estate agent, who told him that Pat and John's house was for sale but not yet listed. The dentist's parents lived in the community; he wanted the house and paid the full amount. The closing was on a Friday. After the agent's cut, Pat and John had $10,000 for the down payment and closed on the Lincroft house on the following Monday. John told Pat that from this time forward, he would travel to whatever job the company gave him and that Pat and the kids would not have to move again. He wanted the family to have roots, and he wanted Pat and the kids to have lasting friendships.

They worked hard to get the Lincroft house in shape. They painted all the rooms. Each year, they borrowed money from their home equity line of credit to make improvements to the house and its surrounding property.

Three years after they moved into the Lincroft house, Pat's mother, Ina, was diagnosed with colon cancer. Pat bathed her, fed her, changed her colostomy bag and addressed all of Ina's needs without ever complaining. She took such good care of her mother day and night that John was worried she would get sick herself. She lost weight, got little sleep and tended to her mother's needs like the nurse she'd once wished to be.

When the school year ended, Pat's younger sisters and brother came to live with Pat and John for the summer. Susan was 18, Richard was 15 and Mary Jane was 13. They said they would figure out what to do next as the summer progressed. Ina did not have a will. She didn't have much in the way of assets; her house was all that was left. Pat and John hired an attorney, Jim Finnerty, to help Ina create a will. For the meeting, Pat and John had to lift Ina out of bed and place her in a chair, since the cancer had taken all the strength from her body. Ina told Jim that she didn't need a will, that her kids would just split whatever money was left from selling the house. Jim was firm and told her that he had seen families fight over money quite often, and he recommended that she think about what she wanted for her three young children. At the time John thought Jim was being rough on Ina, who was so feeble. Jim said he would come back in a day or two after Ina had had time to think it over.

John and Ina realized that Jim was right. When he came back, she had her thoughts together, and Jim recorded her wishes. The next day Jim came back with the will, which Ina signed. After that, she never got out of bed again. John never forgot how Ina's mental strength kept her body alive during that challenging time.

Two weeks later, Ina passed away. Unfortunately, Pat and John were out at dinner when it happened. John had been so concerned for his wife's health that he had suggested a dinner out. Pat had intended to be there when her mother passed, and John felt horrible that she wasn't. The issue came up occasionally at times when their relationship was tested by life's challenges.

Ina was 57. Pat and John were 30 years old at the time. Not only did they have two little girls at home, but now they also had three teenagers. The big house they thought would accommodate their needs into the foreseeable future suddenly became very small. Susan spent much of the summer with them but eventually moved to an apartment in Phillipsburg so she could be closer to her boyfriend. However, she spent most weekends with Pat and John in Lincroft.

Pat's older brother, Jackie, had offered to take one of the younger siblings, but no more than one. Pat was upset and cried to John that she wanted the three of them to stay together. They stayed up late one night discussing the situation. Finally, John told her that the three kids could live with them. This was a very big decision, but John loved Pat deeply and did not want her to be saddened any more than she was already. He had also promised Ina that he would look after her three youngest children. Together, the couple braced themselves to expand their family overnight.

Pat's sister Susan and her husband Wayne were often part of family gatherings.

Pat's sister Mary Jane and her husband Brad attend one of the many Gammino family birthday parties.

Pat's youngest brother Richard takes in the scene at a family wedding.

CHAPTER 13

A Busy Life in Lincroft

OVER THE YEARS, THE LINCROFT HOUSE BECAME the center of activity for all the Gammino kids and the extended family. Shortly after Pat's younger siblings moved in, Pat learned that she was pregnant. It was to be the single most important event that united the younger kids and the older ones. While she was pregnant, her doctor told her she must not have any more children. Pat's petite body had been through four pregnancies, and her legs were showing signs of vein issues.

With this news, John volunteered to have a vasectomy. On the day of the vasectomy, John was so nervous he poured himself a tumbler of Scotch. Pat drove him to the appointment. She waited in the car. They were told the entire procedure would take no more than 30 minutes. When he arrived at the doctor's office, the nurse told him to go into one of the examining rooms and get undressed. "Don't touch anything," she said. John was confused. How could he get undressed and hang up his clothes without touching anything? Recognizing his confusion, the nurse clarified: "Don't touch anything down there." She pointed to his crotch. Now it was abundantly clear what she meant. John got dressed in the paper gown, got on the table as instructed by the nurse, and began to sweat profusely.

Dr. Juarez came into the room with a tray of utensils that were frightening. John looked at them and said, "What are you going to do with them?" The doctor had a great sense of humor, so he just smiled, and this made John even more nervous. Dr. Juarez told John he was going to inject a numbing medication before beginning the procedure. John shuddered, and as the procedure began, he wished he had had two glasses of Scotch instead of one. He closed his eyes and felt a pulling sensation on the right side where the doctor was working. He couldn't look at the devices the doctor was using; it was too scary. When the right side was done, Dr. Juarez said, "Mr. Gammino, as you know, we have two testicles. Right about now you are probably wishing you only had one." Though he later found the doctor's comment to be funny, he did not find it humorous at the time.

When the procedure was finished, John was told to rest over the weekend and not to do anything strenuous, or there could be complications. He was to lie on the couch and relax. As he walked to the car afterward, he felt as though he had been in the doctor's office for an entire day. However, it had only been 35 minutes. Pat started laughing uncontrollably when she saw him walking toward the car. She said he looked like he had just gotten off a horse. John wasn't amused. Later, though, they both laughed about the experience.

Pat loved to laugh at John. He said that whenever anything bad happened to him, she laughed. She said he was exaggerating. So he recounted a story. When she was pregnant with Melissa in Absecon, she wanted John to put a bar in the attic on which to hang out-of-season clothing. She climbed the pull-down staircase with John and sat on a box while John was installing the bar. There was no flooring in the attic, so John had to step on rafters to get his footing.

John slipped and fell between the rafters. Pat was hysterical with laughter. John was hanging on the rafters by his arms, but his body had crashed into the ceiling below. When he managed to get himself back up into the attic, he helped Pat descend the stairs. She then saw that the crash had left a gaping hole in the ceiling, and there was insulation all over their bed. Laughter quickly turned to tears.

Pat admitted that John certainly had a point, but John had one more story to share. "What about the time that I went to work on an icy day and slipped as I was getting into the car?" John said. "I ripped my pants, hurt my shoulder and you couldn't stop laughing." Pat laughed out loud. "Should I continue?" he asked. She shook her head no while still laughing. Their relationship was very special. They could laugh and kid around with each other in a playful way. They made it a point to never go to bed angry.

After one day on the couch, John began to feel better from the procedure and decided to take the girls fishing. He took Maureen and Melissa to a nearby pond. He bent down to bait their hooks, and he was continually squatting to get into the tackle box for hooks, etc. Eventually, he began to feel as if something was wrong. He took the girls home and realized that he had blood in his underwear. He had ignored the doctor's orders and was now suffering the consequences.

Except for a bout with appendicitis, he had never missed a day of work, so on Monday he went into the office even though he still had complications. Sitting in a suit and tie at his desk, he was feeling wet. One of his managers, upon hearing of the problem, went into the ladies' room and got him two Kotex pads. They laughed about it, but it was nothing compared to the laugh that Pat had when she heard about it.

Finally, baby Michael was born. The year was 1975, and it was the first birth John would be able to watch. He was in a chair near the head of Pat's bed, looking into a mirror that showed the birth. The doctor saw the head coming and instructed Pat to push. She pushed and pushed and then the entire head appeared, followed by the little body. Michael's eyes were closed as he exited his comfortable womb and entered the vast room with the glaring lights. It seemed to John that Michael opened his eyes and wondered where the hell he had just landed. It was the most beautiful miracle John had ever witnessed. After the nurse cleaned him up, they placed him in a blanket and handed him to Pat. John was overwhelmed with the magic of the entire experience.

Pat and John loved their kids. They bought the girls a stereo with two microphones. One day the girls asked John to come into their bedroom. They each had a microphone and were playing the song "Celebration." Each was going through their rehearsed choreography. He loved it. They were all happy with their life in Lincroft. The kids were great together and enjoyed their surroundings.

In addition to a plethora of friends, the kids had many animals through the years. There were rabbits, several dogs, a cat, guinea pigs, turtles and hamsters. The family had swelled to include Pat, John, six kids and a bunch of animals. John would often comment that it was like a zoo. Pat turned the house into a home and managed it all, which allowed John to concentrate on his career.

Pat was known to be a talker. She kept in touch with friends and family on the phone when she could not do it in person. She had many friends.

At 4 years old, Melissa was the child most affected by the addition of so many people to the family all at once. Pat obviously had to divide her time among all the children, so Melissa didn't get the attention she wanted from her mother. One day she decided to leave home. She packed a little suitcase and went upstairs to the kitchen, where she found Pat on the phone. Melissa gave Pat a note saying she was running away from home. John had taught her how to make a paper airplane, and that's how she delivered her note. Then she took her suitcase and walked across the cul-de-sac to a neighbor's house.

The neighbor had a dog named Chip. Melissa and Chip were buddies. Melissa decided that while her mother was looking for her, she would hide in Chip's doghouse. It must have seemed like an eternity to a 4-year-old. After 30 minutes, Melissa thought that her mother must be out looking for her by now, so she decided to go home. When she arrived, Pat was still on the phone and hadn't even left her chair. Pat had watched Melissa walk to the neighbor's house and figured she was fine. Melissa's plan didn't work, and she was not happy. Even the act of running away from home didn't give her the attention she wanted from her mother. Pat kidded Melissa about the incident for years. Of course, in later years they both laughed about it, but at the time Melissa did not find it funny!

Around that same time, Melissa came into the house crying on several occasions, saying that one of the little boys in the neighborhood was hitting her. His name was Danny. John took Melissa aside and talked with her. He taught her how to make a fist, ensuring that she put her thumb below her knuckles. He had Melissa practice hitting his hand. He made her do it until he was sure that she knew to throw the punch directly from her chest at the target. Then he told her that if Danny ever hit her again, she should take her fist and punch him right in the nose. That way, Danny would not bother her again. A week later, John came home from work and found Melissa with a big smile on her face. John asked what she was grinning about. She said that Danny had hit her and that she had punched him right in the nose. She said Danny went home crying, and John told her he was very proud of her.

A week or so later, Melissa was bringing her doll carriage into the house. Maureen told her that their mom didn't want the doll carriage inside because the wheels were dirty. Melissa calmly went around the carriage, walked up the steps and punched Maureen in the nose. When John heard about this, he was sure he had created a monster. He had to explain to Melissa that you only do that in self-defense.

Meanwhile, Pat enrolled Mike in a preschool nature program at a place called Poricy Park. One day, Pat suggested that John come along, so he did. The teacher at Poricy Park asked who wanted to go get Charlie. Mike volunteered, and shortly thereafter he came back with a python around his neck. Apparently Charlie was the name of the python. With his deep-seated snake phobia, John did not want to show his fear or his anger. As usual, Pat found it humorous, but it was the last time John would visit the place.

As time progressed, fitting all the kids into the four-bedroom house became a challenge. John remodeled the basement by installing paneling and a tile floor. Although he had no previous experience with remodeling, he did the work himself. The basement became Richard's room. Maureen and Melissa shared a room; Mary Jane had her own room. Michael had the room across the hall from Pat and John's.

Fortunately, John had some help with his next household project; the Mantoni family came for a visit. Bob helped John set up a foundation for a sizable screened-in porch. After Bob left, John finished most of the work himself. The timing wasn't so great, however, because Pat had just brought Michael home from the hospital. John was hammering and sawing and generally making more noise than a mother wanted for a newborn she was trying to get to sleep. However, with the increased family size, the screened porch became the center of activity on many occasions.

The house was like a hotel with revolving doors. Friends of Pat and John frequently stopped by, as did friends of all the kids. At times it was maddening. John would work hard to get the lawn to look nice and Mike would have his friends over to play tackle football and would tear it up. There were many trees that shed leaves. John would try to get the family out to rake, but most often the outdoor work fell to him.

One day when the kids were actually helping John rake, a little rabbit came right up to them and began jumping in the leaves. At one point he laid on his side and allowed the girls to pet him. This was something they had never experienced before. They named him "Sweet Dreams." They fed him, and he returned each day for a few weeks to spend time with them.

One day, he didn't come back, and the girls were so upset that Pat and John bought a new rabbit. It was put in a cage next to a shed. They fed him and took him out of the cage at times. They absolutely loved their new pet.

Another day, their nephew Greg was visiting, and he found a kitten stuck in a tree just behind the back porch. He named her Cali. After Pat called around and couldn't find the owner, Greg's parents let him keep it. Greg loved his new kitten dearly. A few days later, however, Pat found Cali's owners. Greg was devastated but bravely brought her back, holding on to her tightly during the trip to the Gammino house. After Pat put Cali in a carrier, she produced another carrier with a new kitten for Greg (she had visited the animal shelter that morning). Greg was overcome with emotion and eternally grateful for Pat's kindness.

This 1980s photo is from a gathering that included John's nephew Greg and niece Michelle.

John worked all over the state of New Jersey, but fortunately he had a company car. His commute to work was as long as an hour and a half each way. He didn't mind. Weekends were his to enjoy with his family. Pat made the house a home and expanded the family to a community of friends that would stop by at any time. Life was full—so nothing could have prepared John or Pat for what happened next.

CHAPTER 14

The Phone Call

THEN CAME THE THURSDAY THAT WOULD change their lives forever. John was working in his Marlton office when his secretary said, "Your wife is on the phone, and she sounds upset." When John picked up the phone, Pat told him that she had received a call from a policeman in Phillipsburg who was an old friend of theirs. He told her an attorney had called the police station looking for contact information for Pat Morello regarding her father's estate (Morello was Pat's maiden name). The policeman said he knew Pat but would not give the attorney her contact information. Instead, he asked for the attorney's number and said he would give it to Pat.

Pat was crying as she told John, "It's her."

John said, "It's who?"

Pat said again, "It's her."

John realized that she was talking about the daughter they had given up for adoption, and asked Pat how she was so sure.

Pat said, "You know my father doesn't have an estate!" Her father could barely get by financially.

John told Pat to relax and said that he would call the attorney. The attorney's name was Joe Buckley. His office was in Trenton, less than an hour from John's office. John called and said he was returning the call for his wife, Patricia Morello Gammino. Joe said he was sorry, but that he couldn't talk with John until he had permission from Pat. John immediately knew that Pat's instinct was correct. He told Joe that he would have his wife call him.

When Pat called Joe, she said, "I know why you're calling. It is about a young, beautiful woman who was born on December 13, 1961." Joe was shocked and told Pat that she was correct. He said he was an amateur photographer and Lisa, the young lady he was representing, did some modeling for him. He said that when Lisa was 10 years old, she had looked in her mother's filing cabinet and found a letter from the Catholic charity where she had been placed for adoption. The letter was from a nun who told Lisa that her mother and father were too young and did not have the means to care for her. The nun also said that Lisa's mother had cried and cried because she didn't want to give her up, and that the nun had had to take her forcibly from her mother. The letter also said that Lisa's father had won a scholarship to Notre Dame and had gone on to college. This letter created a burning desire in Lisa to find and meet her mother.

Pat told Joe that Lisa had not only found her mother, but also her father. Joe was elated that he had found both parents. Pat told him that he could speak with John, and that John would probably want to meet with him. Pat called John and relayed the conversation she'd had with Joe. John called Joe again and got directions to his office. As soon as he hung up the phone, he was out the door. As he was leaving, he told his secretary that he would not be back the rest of the day. She looked at him and said he was as white as a ghost. She asked if he was okay, and he said yes and thanked her for her concern. He said there was a pressing family matter that he had to take care of right away.

As John drove to Trenton, his mind was racing. He thought of how many times he had wanted to find Lisa to see how she was doing. He wanted to watch her go to school and interact with other kids. Pat would always tell him that he shouldn't do it. She would say, "We don't have the right to interfere in her life." John would counter that he just wanted to see her and that he didn't want to interfere. But Pat was adamant, and he loved her. He knew she had made a great sacrifice for him when she went away to have the baby and eventually give her up for adoption. He respected Pat and her wishes and therefore never reached out to find Lisa. Now they would finally get to meet their daughter, albeit 19 years later.

John was invited into Joe's office. During their long conversation, Joe told John about Lisa discovering the letter and always wanting to find her mom. Lisa didn't know her mother had married her father. This was going to be a pleasant shock for her. Joe showed John a picture of Lisa holding onto a cable and leaning out from a yacht. John immediately saw the resemblance to his daughter Maureen. In the picture, Lisa was in a striped T-shirt and tight shorts, and her blonde hair was flowing in the wind. John unconsciously jumped into father mode and asked Joe what his relationship was with Lisa. Even though Joe assured him it was just model and photographer, John became uneasy.

Joe suggested that they have a meeting the following Sunday in a neutral place. He recommended the Ramada Inn in New Brunswick. It was about midway between Lisa's college in Wayne, New Jersey, and Pat and John's home. They settled on a time of 2:30 p.m.

When John got home, he threw his arms around Pat and hugged her. Both of them were smiling, and both had tears in their eyes. They were finally going to meet their lost daughter.

The days certainly dragged from Thursday to Sunday. On Saturday evening, when John finally got to sit down and read the paper, he looked at the horoscopes. Born on October 29th, he was a Scorpio. His horoscope said, "You are about to meet a long-lost relative." He showed Pat and cut out the horoscope. He was shaken; this had to be a message from God. Now all they could do was wait.

CHAPTER 15

The Meeting

SUNDAY FINALLY ARRIVED. THEY WENT TO church with the kids and took them to breakfast. Pat and John left at around 1:30 for the meeting, and both were very nervous. When they reached the parking lot of the Ramada Inn, John went around the car to get Pat. She was shaking, so he put his arm around her to steady her. As they walked toward the entrance, they saw a young woman in a car with two guys. She bolted out of the car and into their arms. Without a word being spoken, Lisa was in the arms of her biological mother and father for the first time in her adult life. The three of them shed tears of happiness. It was an incredibly touching scene.

They went into the hotel and inquired if Joe Buckley had made a reservation. He had, so they went to the room and began talking. Joe had astutely allowed the meeting to take place without him. At one point he stopped by just to make sure all was well. When he found that it was, he left.

John started the conversation by telling Lisa how much they had wanted to find her but also hadn't wanted to interfere in her life. Lisa recounted the story of finding the letter in her mother's filing cabinet. She said she had always wanted to find her birth mother. Pat explained that neither she nor John wanted to give Lisa up for adoption, but that the parents had all the power back then. John said that his father wanted him to be the first in the family to go to college.

Lisa said that she had no animosity toward anyone. She just wanted to find her mother and go forward. The conversation turned to where Lisa had grown up. It was in Ewing, about 45 minutes away from where Pat and John lived. As Lisa spoke further, she mentioned a priest that was a friend of the family. The priest's name was Father John.

Pat and John looked at each other, and Pat said, "Not Father John Giordano?"

Lisa said, "Yes, do you know him?"

Pat said that she and John had gone to school with Father John, but that Tom Giordano, the priest's brother, was a classmate and friend of theirs. Lisa said that the Giordanos spent holidays with her family and that the family also visited Tom and his wife, Mary Ann. Lisa's parents went to parties at Tom's house in West Long Branch. That meant that Lisa had traveled within half a mile of Pat and John's house in Lincroft. It also meant that Pat and John might have been at parties with Lisa's adoptive parents. Pat and John had a social relationship with Tom and Mary Ann. The coincidences were becoming overwhelming.

Lisa mentioned that Tom and Mary Ann had gone through a divorce, and that her mother worked for an attorney who represented Tom. John then realized there had been another significant incident. During the course of Tom's divorce, Pat and John had invited him to dinner one evening. Tom had excused himself for a few moments to place a call to a woman who worked for his attorney. John looked at Lisa and asked, "Could that have been a call to your mother?"

Lisa said, "It was no doubt my mother."

John pointed to all the close lines of intersection in their lives and the great irony in what they had just discussed. He then handed Lisa the horoscope from the night before, and she was stunned. She asked if she could keep it and John said, "Of course." Before the meeting ended, they traded contact information. John said he would arrange for Lisa to come to the house and meet her sisters and brother. They were all ecstatic.

Pat and John decided to tell the kids about Lisa and take the risk that their reactions might not be pleasant. Maureen was 13, Melissa was 10 and Mike was 5 years old. They decided that Mike was too young to hear the entire story, so they just said that Lisa was a special relative. Mike accepted that.

John called his father and said he would be in the area on business the next day and wanted to stop by to say hello. When he entered the house, Jake said, "You really don't have business here, do you?" John responded honestly that he did not. Jake asked, "Do I need a drink for this?" John replied that they both needed a drink. He poured a glass of wine for each of them. Then he told Jake that their daughter had found them through an attorney.

Jake choked up and said it was his fault entirely. He said there were so many times over the years that he'd wanted to tell John how sorry he was. He said that things could have been worked out differently, but he was the one who didn't allow it. He apologized to John and told him how much he regretted his actions and how much he had thought about it over the years. John finally stopped him, thinking he was going to have a heart attack. Jake was shaking. John said he understood why Jake had made the decisions he'd made and said he didn't want to rehash any of it. He wanted to move forward and have Lisa in their lives. He wanted everybody to try to fill in the void that was left from the situation.

John then asked about his mother's whereabouts. Jake said she was getting her hair done and that he was to pick her up in a short while and then go to lunch. At lunch, when Rose heard John's story, she started shaking and her eyes filled with tears. John told them that he would bring Lisa to meet them in the near future.

John had been transferred from Marlton to headquarters in Newark. The move put his work much closer to Lisa's college. He was happy that this would afford him more time to get to see her. John and Lisa had many dinners together. They talked about everything imaginable, trying to fill in the blanks of 20 years of separation.

John made arrangements to pick up Lisa and take her to the house in Lincroft to meet the rest of the family and stay the weekend. The plan included meeting her younger siblings, as well as Pat's siblings (Susan, Richard and Mary Jane), some of Pat and John's good friends, and John's mother and father. It was a busy weekend. The kids and Lisa bonded instantly.

When they reached Phillipsburg to meet with Rose and Jake, Jake asked for a few minutes alone with Lisa. He told her that he was very sorry for how things had worked out. He told her that she should not blame Pat and John, but that it was him she should blame. Lisa handled herself with wisdom beyond her years and told him that she bore no grudges. She assured him that she was happy to have found an entire family, when she had really only hoped to find her mother. All was good...for a while.

Bob Saccani was Lisa's adoptive father. He agreed to have dinner with Lisa, Pat and John. Bob was a handsome man, well-dressed and affable. He told Pat and John that he was very happy that Lisa had found her birth parents and family. But he said that he did not think it would be possible for them to meet Ann Marie, his wife. He said she suffered from emotional disorders and was prone to bouts of anger. John said that he appreciated the opportunity to meet Bob, and he appreciated the kindness with which he'd handled the situation. John assured him that he and Pat did not want to interfere in their relationship with Lisa, but they hoped it would grow to be a special relationship that was not intrusive into Lisa's adoptive family. All left the dinner feeling good.

The next time John had dinner with Lisa, she said she felt guilty about not telling her mother and wanted to go ahead and tell her now. John saw this as a potentially inflammatory situation, given what Bob had said at dinner. Lisa's description of Ann Marie was even harsher than Bob's. But John could foresee that Lisa was going to do this despite his and Bob's reservations. He told Lisa that guilt was a heavy matter. He said there might be a day when it caused her to question her new relationship with him and the rest of the family. He told her that someday she would be an adult living on her own, and she would then be able to make her own decisions about her relationship with her birth family.

Lisa went ahead and told her mother about finding her biological parents. Ann Marie became enraged and heaped a huge load of guilt on Lisa. She told Lisa that she had no loyalty and no respect for all that her mother had done for her. Mental abuse was something Ann Marie was reportedly an expert at delivering. It drove Lisa to distance herself from Pat and John and their family and friends. They didn't know if they would ever reunite.

The smiles were wide the first weekend Lisa came to visit her biological family.

Pat and Lisa bonded instantly.

CHAPTER 16

A Test of Patience

THE KIDS ALL LOVED GROWING UP IN LINCROFT. It was a place where they could ride their bikes wherever they wanted, for the most part. They had many friends with many activities. Mike joined the Pop Warner football team known as the Chargers. He spent several years in different positions and was a very versatile player. He was a fullback, a quarterback, a receiver and a linebacker. John would play the theme song from Rocky when he drove Mike to football practice, which would get Mike revved up and ready. He was also a baseball pitcher with a great fastball who often had fans on the edges of their seats. Sometimes his throwing would be wild and he would walk three batters, loading the bases. But then just as often, he would strike out the next three.

When Mike was in sixth grade, his school took the kids on a trip to the Pocono Mountains. Pat, who worked at the Lincroft School that Mike attended, suggested that John volunteer as a chaperone, and he agreed. All the mothers were happy that John was going, for they knew he would keep their kids in line.

When the group arrived, all were assigned to various cabins. John was in cabin 34, which would be recorded in posterity, though John did not know that at the time. There were nine kids in his cabin, including a few known for being mischievous.

The first day, the kids played ball and had a lot of physical activity. Afterward, John took the first shower and discovered that the valve was broken, so some cold water came out of the showerhead while some hot water came out of the faucet. You had to jump around so you wouldn't burn your feet from the scalding water and/or freeze from the frigid shower water. It was quite the ordeal. He explained it to the kids so they wouldn't get hurt. When all were finished with their showers, they headed to the dining hall for dinner. The kids were happy and frisky, but for the most part they were reasonably well-behaved.

After dinner, it was time for a fossil hunt. As they moved down the trail, they passed a bench. All around the bench were juice boxes that some group had just thrown on the ground. Naturally, one of the kids decided it would be fun to get onto the bench and jump down on a juice box. So he did, and the grape juice exploded all over John. When John turned to see which little devil was responsible, he found himself looking directly at his son. Mike looked at his dad sheepishly, not knowing what John was going to say. John just shook his head, knowing that he would have to take another painful shower. That evening, the kids were so riled up that they didn't sleep until John finally raised his voice and they knew he meant business.

On the second day, one of the kids in John's group, David, found a snake and was swinging it in a circle above his head. John, with his terrible phobia for snakes, told David to put the snake down. David didn't listen until John yelled at him. John was inwardly upset but outwardly calm, and seriously sorry he had volunteered to chaperone. That night he learned that the teachers were getting together and had brought alcohol. He hadn't brought any, and he was very grateful that they shared theirs.

That night, another kid, Kevin, was up most of the night horsing around. John was sure that the devil had gotten into these kids, and he was doomed to a lousy night's sleep again.

On day three, the kids were taken to a lake to go fishing. When they arrived, John led a safety discussion. He told them they had to be 20 feet apart. He said that he would be there if they needed him for tackle or bait or to take a fish off the hook. He also told them that when he blew the whistle, that meant to stop. He meant business.

John helped each kid learn how to cast the line. He gave them all the appropriate warnings about making sure no one was nearby and not to cast in places where their hook was sure to get stuck.

The kids began to catch fish in large numbers and were having a great time. John blew the whistle when it was time to go back to the bus. Of course one kid, Jimmy, decided to make one more cast. When he drew the pole back, the lure went into Mark's nose. It was a treble hook with barbs. John was very calm (on the surface) and told both boys not to move. He took the pole from Jimmy and created a lot of slack in the line. He told Mark that everything was going to be fine. He was praying that the treble hook had not lodged in Mark's nose. He was thinking he didn't know how far the nearest hospital was, and that he had to use extreme care. John carefully took hold of the lure, gave it a slight turn, and it fell out of Mark's nose. John breathed a huge sigh of relief.

The next morning, the bus left for home. When they pulled into the Lincroft School parking lot, all the moms were there. When John exited the bus, they all asked if their kids had been well-behaved. John simply told them that he didn't want to see their kids for at least three weeks. The mothers all looked at each other and then John said firmly again, "At least three weeks." John told Pat the stories, and as usual she laughed hysterically. John laughed too, but he never again volunteered for a school trip.

Lincroft was a small bedroom community. Many of the residents traveled via train or bus to New York City to work. It was a small-town environment where everyone knew each other.

Therefore, when the neighbors recommended a house painter, Pat hired him to paint their house. His name was Ronnie, and he had been in a car accident that injured his brain. Pat told John she wanted to give him a chance, even though he was known to do some crazy things. Ronnie was living in his car because his parents had moved away. Because he had cash flow issues, Pat gave Ronnie a $500 upfront payment so he could purchase the paint and other things he needed.

Ronnie didn't show up for the next five days. Pat was not happy with him. When he finally showed up to work, he asked Pat if she had seen the Yankee game a few nights before when a guy was shown on TV running across the field. She said that she had not. Ronnie then explained that he had been scalping tickets and the police were after him, so he had jumped onto the field to get away. The police caught him and put him in jail.

As usual, Pat privately found this to be hysterical, but she told Ronnie he had to be more responsible. When she told John, he just shook his head. He was really worried about the quality of Ronnie's work, and he thought that Pat had made a big mistake in hiring him.

John would get up early to commute to work in Newark. One morning around 6 a.m., he went into the bathroom to take a shower. He took off his pajamas and was about to get in. However, it was a bright morning, so he wanted to look out at the weather as he showered. When he raised the blinds,

John's brother Jim and his wife Gina have been married for 28 years.

there was Ronnie on a ladder smiling and waving to him. John was livid, but Pat thought it was funny.

Ronnie had a big black dog that he would often bring with him. Twice, the dog went after John when he arrived home from work. John sternly told Ronnie never to bring the dog again. Ronnie apologized and said he would comply.

One day, Ronnie accidentally knocked out a window in the living room while moving his ladder. He told Pat that he would replace the window before the end of the day. That day, again, Ronnie had his dog with him. Pat told Ronnie he had better get the dog out of there soon, because John would be coming home from work. Ronnie didn't listen and was in the process of installing the new pane of glass when John pulled into the driveway. As the dog moved toward John, Ronnie jumped off the ladder to grab him, and the pane of glass crashed onto the surface below. John and Pat were able to laugh about it, but John told her that she was as crazy as Ronnie for hiring him.

Pat was in charge of the house and made it a wonderful place for the family to live and for family and friends to visit. On most weekends and holidays, the house was more like a hotel. John's mother and father came most weekends to see the kids. Jim was often there as well. In later years, when Jim was married, both he and his wife would stay there. It was not uncommon for Pat to have 13 people for several days. She always had great energy and handled the situation well. John would do a lot of cooking on the grill and the crowd would often eat on the porch that he had built. The ease with which Pat and John enjoyed their home made it all the more difficult when it came time for them to consider leaving it.

CHAPTER 17

The Impossible Dilemma

AS A RESULT OF A REORGANIZATION, NEW JERSEY
Bell became a subsidiary of Bell Atlantic, which was located in Washington, D.C. John believed his next assignment would be at the headquarters in D.C. At the time, Maureen and Melissa were in high school. On numerous occasions at dinner, John would bring up the subject of moving to D.C. No one in the family wanted to hear it. John told them that if they wanted his career to continue to advance, that's where he would likely end up.

Pat and the girls made it clear that they were not leaving New Jersey. John said if that were true, he might have to look for another job. They would always respond that he would be crazy to do that, since he would lose his benefits and his pension. He would also point out the reality that if he left the company, they might not have the same lifestyle. The kids didn't want to be poor, didn't want to move and didn't want John to change jobs. It was seemingly an impossible dilemma, and John realized that he had to do something to break the contradictions that they were imposing on him.

It was 1983, and John was head of the Public Communications Division of New Jersey Bell, which meant he managed a $300 million business with 88,000 payphones across the state. As had been the case twice before, he was responsible for working with the executives and the departments to coordinate the corporate reorganization. At the same time, he also had to manage the corporate construction and engineering staffs. So there he was, as busy as he could ever have imagined, with no time to look for another position outside the company.

It was a time when the entire fabric of the "telephone company," as Americans knew it, was being pulled apart. John decided that the company needed to learn more about the world of competition, which heretofore it had never had to face.

Tim Schilling, who reported to John, was the head of the Fiber Optics division. He was a different kind of manager — a free spirit. He challenged conventional ideas, and he was naturally curious about things. One day, John reassigned Tim from fiber optics and asked him to take a temporary, unofficial role. He tasked Tim with exploring the external competitive telecom and technology world. What was the company going to be facing? He was concerned that no one in the company was considering this critical business angle.

Tim absolutely loved his new role, and it turned out to be one of the best decisions John had made in his career. They unearthed a treasure trove of information about this new business world. They cataloged companies that were offering new ways of doing things. They learned about new technologies. They learned about entrepreneurial start-ups.

Some people at New Jersey Bell thought John had lost his mind because he was spending so much time on this matter. Then one day the New Jersey Public Utilities Commission asked New Jersey Bell what risks there were from the new competitive world the company would be operating in. No one had the answers. Finally, John and Tim's work was recognized for its importance. John created a slide presentation and called it *Staar Waors* (Satellite, Terrestrial and Advanced Radio versus What About Old Reliable Service). In it, he examined the new world of technology and products, as well as risks and opportunities.

John's boss, Cliff DeAnna, loved the presentation and asked him to present it to the division management team. It was an eye-opener. John would never forget the first comment he received when he was finished with the slide show. One of the participants said in a tone of naiveté, shock and extreme discomfort: "You are talking about RISK!" John assured him that he was correct! John thought Cliff was going to fall out of his chair.

John was working three jobs and was as busy as he could possibly be, but he was loving what he was doing. Nonetheless, he knew at some point it would all end, since his family wasn't willing to move.

As if often does, fate intervened at just the right moment. One day, John saw an ad in the *Wall Street Journal* for a company called Robert Jamison Associates (RJA). The firm offered a book about how busy executives could successfully change jobs. He ordered it and read it as soon as it arrived. It sold him on the idea that with his limited time, he needed someone to help market him. RJA was the perfect organization to do that.

The firm interviewed John, learned about his management experience and accomplishments, and then prepared marketing materials that would be used to sell his talents to the marketplace. When John reviewed the résumé they had prepared, he told them they had made a mistake. They showed him as Chief Executive of the New Jersey Bell Public

Communications Division. John said, "I am not a chief executive. I am a division manager."

In the ensuing conversation, the RJA rep grew frustrated. He finally said, "You told me you have profit and loss responsibility. You said you have very little supervision. You said you are responsible for marketing, finance and operations. Is that correct?"

John said, "Yes, that is correct."

The RJA rep told John he had to step outside of his body and look at himself as a product. He asked, "Do you remember the commercial that said, 'Arrid Extra Dry is unsurpassed at stopping wetness'?"

John nodded.

He asked, "How much Arrid Extra Dry do you think we would have sold if we'd said 'Arrid is nothing special, it's just like all the other deodorants'? You are a product, and we are selling you via your résumé. Your modesty needs to be removed from this process."

It took some time for this to gestate within John's psyche. He had to overcome 13 years of Catholic school training in humility. Later on, he would be very glad he had learned this lesson, because otherwise he would never have attracted a single client when he started his own consulting business.

In the month that followed, 500 letters were mailed to recruiters, companies and influential people. This produced 10 companies that were interested in talking with him. With the RJA training, John turned that into three job opportunities—none of which were closer than Washington, D.C. He spent a lot of money to discover that his talents were marketable, but the issue of moving was obviously still a deal-breaker for his family.

Faced with this new roadblock, John began thinking about starting his own business. The idea terrified Pat, because her father had worked tirelessly as a business owner his whole life and had died of a heart attack at age 54. The kids were similarly negative, thinking surely the family would be poor. Undaunted, John was getting increasingly excited about the idea. The biggest downside was that he would lose the family health care, life insurance and other benefits that he enjoyed at Bell. He was having a serious internal debate about what to do. One day he took pen to paper and laid out the pluses and the minuses as best he could. Even that exercise didn't provide a clear answer.

One day while driving to work, he had a eureka moment. His benefits were primarily for his family. If he died, they would get a death benefit of a year of his salary and double or triple indemnity if it were the result of an accident. They would also get his life insurance. With the exception of health insurance, he didn't get the benefits; they did. It was at this point that he decided to break the mental logjam. He was going to give his family their desire to live in New Jersey, but in return they would have to give up the benefits that made them feel comfortable. John gave up the comfort of a corporate career and decided to pursue the option of starting his own business.

You know that expression "leap and the net will appear"? That's just what happened. Right after John made his big decision, New Jersey Bell decided to offer an early retirement incentive of a year's salary. Although it was without a doubt the riskiest move he ever made, John took it. It was the first time the company had ever made such an offer, and it certainly wasn't designed to provide an incentive for 39-year-old management employees to leave. But the loophole was there, and John took it against the advice of many who thought he had a bright career at Bell. When his peers and others learned of his decision to leave, many of them said, "You have balls." Cliff DeAnna, for whom John had the highest regard, said, "You will be successful. You are a problem-solver. The solutions you provide will be welcome in the marketplace." John appreciated that vote of confidence, though he still had some reservations about his decision.

The day John left New Jersey Bell headquarters in Newark, he had the urge to jump in the air and click his heels, along with the urge to throw up. He had never had such a feeling before. It wouldn't be the last time that such conflicting emotions took over his mind and body.

During his job search that year, John met a man named John Meggitt. John and his wife, Dorothy, had founded and managed a company called Prophet 21. The company manufactured computer systems for the distributor marketplace. John Meggitt was from IBM and had been a Rhodes scholar. The couple was very welcoming and courteous, and they had many discussions about the possibility of John joining their company.

John never forgot the advice Meggitt gave him when he said he was considering going into his own consulting business. He said, "You and I are from large companies. Those companies deal in hundreds of millions and billions of dollars. When you are in your own business, you deal in dollars and cents. If I can give you one piece of advice, it would be to learn small business on someone else's nickel for six months before you go into your own business."

This was the best advice John could have received. He adapted the RJA system in an effort to find a local company with whom he could obtain a position and learn the ways of small business. He responded to an ad for a computer programmer and asked the contact to forward his information to the CEO of the company. He was ready to test that advice.

CHAPTER 18

The Life-Changing Leap

JOHN'S STRATEGY WORKED; THE CEO CONTACTED him. John became the president and CEO of Dimis Micro Systems Inc. (DMS) in Ocean, New Jersey, and he was happy because his commute was now only 15 minutes long. He left New Jersey Bell on Thursday, November 30, 1983, and on Monday morning, December 4, 1983, he was president of a computer software company. The company packaged its software with personal computers and therefore sold turnkey systems.

John Meggitt was right. John had a lot to learn. He met with the employees of the new company, which was based in Tempe, Arizona. He was anxious to see how his 17 years of managing a technical business at Bell would hold up in the hotly competitive personal computer business. Through experience, he learned that it might take as long as six months to become comfortable in his new role. He was once again a sponge, learning about the business, soaking up every bit of knowledge he could.

He recalled another lesson from his friend John. He was at his desk wondering why he had so much time on his hands when it occurred to him that he didn't have to attend any meetings unless he called one. And he didn't have to answer any memos unless he generated the need. It was quite interesting to find out how much of his time in the big corporation had been taken up by such things. John had many ideas that he wanted to explore, and he was thinking he would call in the staff one morning to discuss them. Then he laughed and realized—he *was* the staff. The list was shortened quickly, and the priorities were soon very clear.

John hired a marketing executive and an engineering executive for DMS, and together they relocated the business from Tempe to Ocean. They developed a business plan for integrating hardware and software, and a path forward for the company in the new competitive world of personal computers.

At the time, there were rumors that AT&T would be getting into the computer business (AT&T had been the parent company of New Jersey Bell). There were also rumors that IBM would be entering the telecommunications business. The clash of the titans was seemingly on the horizon. Major consulting firms had convinced IBM that its experience in computing could be used to put smart switches in the telecom market and compete with AT&T. They also convinced AT&T that its smart switches could be modified to perform computing tasks in competition with IBM.

John took a shot at sending a letter to the CEO of AT&T and explaining in one page how he was a former employee and how he could help with their entry into the computer business. Because he had only just left New Jersey Bell, he knew the buzzwords and language that would resonate with them. Soon after the letter was sent, Tom Berry, an A&T CFO, called him and asked for a meeting. The night before the meeting, John was sitting at the dining room table with Pat wondering what he was going to present. His new company had a software program to automate tax preparation for accountants. When John and his team put the business plan together, they accumulated a good deal of information about the accounting marketplace. There he was with few resources, but with an awesome software program that ran on a PC.

John gave considerable thought to a strategy to present at the meeting, but he hadn't had time to prepare a professional presentation. In the end, he decided the best way to illustrate his concept was to draw a horizontal bar and a vertical bar in the shape of an upside-down T on a yellow legal pad. Pat laughed nervously, thinking that wasn't much of a presentation for an AT&T CFO. Pat also trusted John's business instincts, and she encouraged him to follow through with his idea.

When John walked into Tom Berry's office, Tom pulled out John's letter, which he had highlighted in places. John knew then that he had Tom's attention. Tom said, "So you are the guy that is going to solve all of AT&T's problems." John said, "I suspect that person doesn't exist, but I can help you with your entry into the computer business."

Tom replied, "Tell me more." John said it wasn't rocket science. Essentially, IBM was to the computer industry what AT&T was to telecommunications. Each company had significant power in its marketplace.

John then offered an alternative to a frontal attack on IBM's business. Tom was interested. John said that the accounting marketplace to which his company's software was targeted would be a good match for AT&T's personal computer launch. It could be sold with hardware and software as a system to the accounting vertical market. John had his statistics about how many firms there were and the relative sizes of those firms, and he said the vertical line on his pad represented

the accounting vertical market. He then explained that the
horizontal line represented the millions of small businesses
that rely on their accountants for business and financial advice.
He explained that if AT&T could dominate the accounting
market, it could then influence the decisions of the millions
of small businesses. In those days, small businesses frequently
consulted their accountants on key decisions. He also said that
AT&T could then capitalize on establishing communications
service between the accountants and their small business
customers. With this plan, AT&T could sneak into the market
under the radar screen and avoid a major confrontation with
IBM while building a strong relationship with accountants
and small businesses.

Tom looked at John for what seemed like an inordinate
amount of time. He finally said, "John, that is brilliant."
He summoned his comptroller out of a meeting and to his
office. He wanted the comptroller to set up a meeting with
his accountants to be sure that the DMS software program
met all the appropriate accounting standards. John left the
meeting excited, mostly because he sensed Tom's enthusiasm.

On the day of the meeting, John and one of his technical
reps arrived early, anticipating that they would be meeting
with just a few AT&T accountants. Incredibly, however, 17
accountants attended the meeting. That was just the first
shock of the day. The second would be the nature of the
questions the accountants asked. Why are you running this
on a PC? Does it run on a mainframe or a minicomputer?
Where is your laser printer? *Blah, blah, blah*, thought John,
who explained that the purpose of the meeting was for them
to determine if the software program met all the appropriate
accounting standards. Unfortunately, they were more interested
in peripheral questions and discussion. John left the meeting
very disappointed.

When he called Tom and explained what happened, Tom was mortified and apologized. He said that he wanted to get John in front of his marketing organization. By the time all of that transpired, John was approaching his planned departure from DMS. His successor would have to navigate the AT&T bureaucracy. John always had a high regard for Tom and his ability to see through the fog of that giant organization and recognize opportunity. Sadly, an AT&T personal computer was never mated to the DMS software, and AT&T went on to spend a fortune trying to compete directly with IBM. Billions were reportedly lost. John was sure it was not for a lack of effort on Tom's part.

During this same time period, John and Pat received a visit from Ed Sheridan, Pat's former boss and an entrepreneur in his own right. He and his brothers had started Sheridan Printing Company in their basement and now had 300 employees. Ed was quite the character. He loved to drink Seagram's VO and tell stories. On this particular visit, John filled him in on all that was going on at DMS. Ed floated the idea of helping John secure the financing to buy the business. He then said, "Why don't you bring your marketing person and your business plan to our office next week. We are looking for investments."

John said, "No way."

Ed was perplexed.

John explained, "This is my risk, and I wouldn't even consider involving friends in such a risky venture."

Ed told John it was strictly business and convinced him to take the meeting. John agreed, albeit reluctantly.

After the meeting, Ed and his staff reviewed the plan and got back to John right away. Ed asked how much money would be needed to buy the business. John guessed $300,000 to $500,000, because it was a very small company. Ed invited

John to a meeting with his banker. John could not believe it was happening at all, much less so quickly.

After John's presentation to the banker, Ed said he wanted to back the purchase of the business with a guarantee from his company. The banker said it was too risky, but then Ed reminded him about their joint history: At one point, the banker had told him that Sheridan Printing was in such bad financial shape that it couldn't even file for Chapter 11 bankruptcy. Since that time, Ed had placed a lot of money with the bank. He told the banker that either the bank would provide the loan to John or Ed would take his money elsewhere.

Again, John was shocked by the ways of the entrepreneur. The banker was nervous, Ed was excited, and John was impressed. John suggested an interim step to bring about what he thought would be a sound resolution of the conflict between Ed and his banker. John said it would take some additional scrutiny on his part to see if the company was actually worth buying. He told them he needed to look at the inventory and receivables in depth before he would be able to answer the question definitively. Ed agreed to wait.

After a very thorough review, John decided the company's major asset was its software program, and that was what they should buy, for a price of $100,000. The banker agreed to loan John the money for the offer. However, the chairman of DMS' parent company declined the offer, saying the program was worth much more than that. The next day, John submitted his resignation.

Ed wasn't through with John yet. He asked how much John needed to start his own consulting firm. John told him he had no idea. Ed said he wanted John to have a line of credit so that he would have a cushion in case he needed it. This was one entrepreneur to another. He knew better than John did that John would need startup cash, so he arranged a $100,000 line of credit with his banker. John used $20,000 to start the business, paid it back within the first year, and never borrowed another penny. He was always grateful to Ed for his support and his generosity.

Before leaving DMS, John received a call from Bill Clancey, a longtime friend, who asked if John had read the *Wall Street Journal* that day. He had read it, but he'd missed the ad that Bill was referencing. It was about a company in Los Angeles named National Pay Telephone, and they were looking for investors. Bill suggested they might need a consultant and that John should give them a call.

John left DMS at the end of June and became a "consultant" for the first time in his life. He wasn't even sure he knew what that meant. He was about to find out.

CHAPTER 19

Do or Die

P AT WAS NERVOUS. JOHN HAD LEFT HIS SECURE
Bell career after 17 years and then had become president
of a computer company. Now he was a consultant on his own
and had no income or clients. John set up a small office at
home. The kids had just left school for the summer and were
ready for fun. Their father, meanwhile, was on a mission to
develop a business.

He made a list of everyone he thought might be influential
in helping him develop clients; he ended up with 70 names.
Most days, he would go into his office at 8 a.m. and (except
for lunch) would not come out until 5:30 or 6 p.m. The kids
asked Pat, "What does dad do in there all day?" They made
lots of noise and had many friends over. From time to time,
John would ask them to be quiet because he was on the phone.
It was difficult to project a professional image when loud kids'
voices could be heard in the background. Therefore, John
made many lunch and breakfast appointments. He decided
that if he was going to make his business a success, he should

make a list of all the areas in which he had experience. Then he separated out the things he actually liked to do. He worked with Sheridan Printing to create a logo, stationery, business cards and a trifold brochure. He named his company John Richard Associates (JRA). Richard was his middle name.

John worked his way through his list of 70 contacts. Bill Clancey was working with AT&T International and introduced John to the manager of the company's international consulting business. The company routinely hired former AT&T and Bell personnel to work on big consulting projects. John had several meetings with him and with others at AT&T, but there were no immediate openings.

About two weeks into his new venture, the ad from the *Wall Street Journal* made it to the top of John's pile. There it was—National Pay Telephone, a new company competing in a business that did not yet exist. It was formed in anticipation of the pay telephone business becoming deregulated from the monopoly phone companies. It was expected that the payphone industry would soon be allowing competition, which created opportunities for entrepreneurs.

While reading the ad, John reflected on when he had managed the public communications business (i.e. payphones). Of all the jobs he had had at Bell, managing this division was one of his biggest thrills. He had turned a sleepy little division into a profit-making venture and morphed it from a monopoly model into a P&L (profit and loss) business. Thanks to the approval of company officers, John had been on his way to testing the competitive waters within this microcosm of the company. Bell Public Communications was thereby formed.

John and his team had learned many lessons about the market and about the changes required in thinking, strategies, and management of this business segment. To begin with, he had revenue data extracted for the top 100 phones and the bottom 100 phones. He'd sent the marketing staff out with Polaroid cameras to collectively inspect the list of 200. He'd examined the expense side as well, and found many areas where capital and expense dollars were being wasted. The division learned fast and changed fast. The experience had been exhilarating, putting his business senses on fire. It was as if he were running a totally separate business.

John had also wanted to instill a competitive entrepreneurial spirit into the techs who were union members, and who had for years been operating on a premise of only doing a certain amount of work in a day. When a repair tech was finished with a job, he or she might be given the next job clear across town. This seemed ludicrous and a colossal waste of time, so John had created a new system. He had his staff divide the state into territories. Techs were assigned to each territory to perform both installation and maintenance tasks. John had explained that each of them was to be the face of the phone company. They could take credit for all that went well. Conversely, they would be liable for all that didn't go well. He challenged them.

Some of the management team thought John had lost his mind. They thought the entire team would be in trouble for throwing out measurement systems that had been in place for decades. But they soon got on board and overcame their fears, especially when they saw results that AT&T compiled from all of its companies. NJ Bell's Public Communications business had risen to the top in nearly every category.

Of course, that was all behind John now, but he wanted to achieve the same success on his own.

He took a deep breath and called the number in the ad. He reached the Public Relations Vice President, Hartley Lord. They exchanged pleasantries and discussed what National Pay Telephone was trying to accomplish. Hartley explained that there was this gigantic market that was about to be opened to competition for the first time and that his firm was preparing to become a major player in this new pay telephone business.

It was at that point that John's Robert Jamison Associates training kicked in. John said things about himself that would have made the nuns in his Catholic school think he was an egomaniac. He violated all the rules they'd taught him about humility and embraced all the new things he had learned from RJA.

He launched into a presentation of his accomplishments at Bell. He said he had managed 88,000 pay telephones and in two years' time helped the division grow from a $190 million business to a $300 million business. He said he knew how to improve profitability and reduce pitfalls and that Hartley needed John more than he knew. John said so many things about himself that it was so out of character for him to say, that he was waiting for Hartley to hang up. Instead, Hartley was ecstatic. He said, "You are exactly what we need. I will have our president call you."

After the call, John found Pat on the back porch and told her about his lack of humility. She laughed. She was nervous about this new venture but chose not to say much about it since it allowed the family to stay in New Jersey.

Over the next few weeks, John and Ross Sheer, the president of National Pay Telephone, had discussions about the possibility of working together. At the same time, John's former colleague and friend, Tim Schilling, told him about a Japanese company that was looking for help getting into the U.S. fiber optics market. John exchanged some correspondence with the firm and began trying to cultivate the relationship.

At this point in the game, John decided he needed to move into an actual office. He subleased some space from an accountant he knew. He also hired his first executive assistant, Debbie, from DMS.

On his first day in the office, John read in AT&T's newsletter that the company's chairman had said it would be looking into vertical markets after losing $2 billion in the computer business. John wanted to scream! He imagined that Tom Berry had tried to carry the yellow pad strategy forward but had failed until the loss of billions occurred.

On his fourth day in the office, a Thursday, John received a call from AT&T International saying it had the perfect consulting gig for him. He would be working with a team of professionals that were preparing a proposal for revamping the telecommunications network of an entire country. John would be working with nine staff members, both retired and active.

John was stoked, but then came the combination of punches that nearly floored him. The consultancy would last five or six weeks and would be located in Bangkok, Thailand, and they wanted him to leave on Saturday—literally three days away. John responded that he was very interested but could not possibly go on Saturday. He asked for 24 hours to get back to them so that he could rearrange some commitments and client matters. They agreed.

John nearly fainted after hanging up the phone. He had just rented and furnished office space, hired an assistant, and now he was going to have to leave his wife in charge of not only a family, but also a business. He knew this was going to be a very difficult dinner conversation.

He managed to regain his composure and decided it was time for him to meet in person with Ross Sheer, who was in California. Ross agreed, and John asked if Ross was going to pay for his trip. Ross responded, "I've also been a consultant, so I'll make you a deal. If I hire you, I will pay for your trip. If I don't hire you, you pay for your trip." John agreed. They decided to meet at LAX airport on the following Monday.

John was on a roll. He decided he should try to meet with the Japanese company ASAP as well. Saturday was the only day the Japanese executive could meet, so John agreed to the meeting. He then called AT&T and said that he could go to Thailand on Monday, but that he had to stop in Los Angeles first. He asked if that could be arranged. They said yes. He was told to be at AT&T International in the morning to sign the contract and receive the necessary vaccinations. John covered the risk of Ross not hiring him and managed to get the weekend to prepare his wife and family for his departure. It was both exhilarating and nerve-racking.

While John was at the AT&T office, his contacts gave him a three-inch-thick book titled *Doing Business in Thailand*. He was sure it would cure his inability to sleep on the plane, and he surely didn't have time to read it over the weekend.

John prepared his proposal for National Pay Telephone, the first one he had done on his own. He showed it to a colleague, who immediately said, "It's good, but double your price!" John was very surprised. Even though his colleague didn't have a lot of experience in the telecom industry, he knew what the Big 8 accounting firms charged, and even if John doubled his price, it would still be under those prices. He did as he was told.

John hired two consultants to keep things together for him while he was gone. If a contract was signed with National Pay Telephone, someone would have to oversee the work. John assured them he would make it worth their while.

On Saturday, he drove to the designated restaurant to meet the representative from the Japanese company, Mr. Wasumi. As he was driving, he wondered how he would recognize the man. It then occurred to him that he might be the only Asian at a restaurant that catered to truck drivers in New Jersey. He was correct.

After John and Mr. Wasumi had exchanged pleasantries, John asked, "How can I be of help?"

His colleague responded, "We will have a drink!"

During the ensuing small talk, John's trip to Asia came up. Mr. Wasumi told John that there were many coup d'états in Thailand. John was already so overwhelmed with all he had to do before Monday that this news made his stomach churn. Mr. Wasumi then said, "Don't worry—they are usually peaceful coups." John was not comforted.

He really wanted to get things moving, so he said again, "Mr. Wasumi, how can I be of service to you?"

Mr. Wasumi replied, "We will have lunch!"

After lunch, John gave Mr. Wasumi his brochure, and Mr. Wasumi gave him the annual report for Nissho Iwai Corporation. John was shocked to see a number in the hundreds of billions. At first, he thought he was looking at Japanese yen, but further reading revealed he was looking at U.S. dollars. He was dining with a representative of Japan's third-largest trading company! Nissho Iwai represented chemical companies, fiber optic companies, telecommunications companies, cigarette companies and others.

Mr. Wasumi then took out a business card and wrote some contact information on it. He said, "Mr. Gammino, when you're through with your visit to Thailand, contact this man, Mr. Motsumoto. You tell him that Wasumi wants you to go to Tokyo to visit our plants. When you come back, we will talk!" John was very happy that he would get the chance to meet with Nissho Iwai in Tokyo and to have this contact with such a large and prestigious company. He was also thinking that he couldn't tell Pat that after his five or six weeks in Thailand, he had to go to Japan for some unknown duration.

As he drove home, John had the very mixed feelings of immense accomplishment, primal fear, total excitement, and disappointment that he would have to be away from his family for such an extended period.

He had managed fiber optics for a short time at Bell, but he certainly wasn't comfortable with his depth of knowledge. Therefore, his friend Tim Schilling gave him a crash course at a bar one afternoon. Tim was a great teacher and drew things out on a cocktail napkin. Afterward, John was comfortable enough to at least carry on a conversation about fiber optics with Nissho Iwai.

John's family was having a hard time with it all, and, in particular, Pat was upset about how long he would be gone and that she would have to watch over his office and his assistant while he was gone.

John didn't know if there were phones in Bangkok that would permit him to call at will, or if he would have to get in line with others. They agreed that he would call on Wednesdays. The time difference was 12 hours, a real challenge. They also agreed that the family would go to the office on Wednesdays so that he could talk with his assistant and his consultants as well.

John left Monday morning. Pat and the kids were crying in the driveway when the car service pulled away. John was incredibly conflicted. Was he doing the right thing by going away for this long? How would they survive if he didn't take the AT&T opportunity? If he had stayed at Bell, they would be crying because they had to move. He finally convinced himself that there was no choice and that he had to do it. This was the chance to make the new business a reality. Eventually, he calmed down and convinced himself that traveling halfway around the world, to work with people he didn't know, in a country that was very foreign to him, to work on a project that he didn't yet understand, was all a part of the process. He would remain calm and take the new experiences in stride. This mind control helped him avoid a complete nervous breakdown!

He boarded the plane in Newark and traveled on the first leg of his journey to Los Angeles. He had reserved a room at the Admirals Club at LAX to meet Ross Sheer. When they met, it didn't take long for them to get deeply engaged in Ross's view of the telecommunications industry, the breakup of AT&T, and his company's opportunity to capture significant market share of the yet-to-be-deregulated pay telephone business.

Having managed that business at Bell, and having dissected the revenues and costs, John was comfortable with the discussion. It was disconcerting, however, to hear Ross talk about the cash business he was about to enter. John knew that 60 to 65 percent of the revenue came from noncash sources such as calling card, collect and third-party-billed calls. Ross and John got into a verbal jousting contest over the nature of the cash and noncash parts of the business. John's instinct, which he followed, was to cut the conversation short and let Ross know that they had different views and therefore it wouldn't make sense to work together. Ross smiled and said, "I agreed with you all along. I was just testing your knowledge."

Chagrined, John replied, "In that case, I brought a proposal for how we might work together." When he got to the fee section, John held his breath.

Ross held out his hand and said, "You aren't cheap, but you aren't the most expensive consultant I ever hired either." He signed both copies and agreed to send a retainer of $10,000 to John's office.

Given that his business was still so young, John was surprised, relieved and delighted to have signed his second client contract. He told Ross he would be gone for about a month and that his colleagues would handle matters in the interim.

John called in from a payphone and told his colleague the good news. The colleague was incredulous that John had landed the contract. He said, "Wait a minute. You mean you got the contract you showed me, and you had never met that man before?" He was in disbelief and didn't think the check would ever arrive.

John also had a gut-wrenching call with Pat, who was crying and saying she missed him already. He knew he had to remain steadfast. As he left for the next leg of his trip to Bangkok, he was amazed at what had just happened. He ordered a drink and reflected on the greatness of America. He was testing his abilities in the marketplace and living the American dream. Wow!

Chapter 20

A Brave New World

THANK GOODNESS FOR BUSINESS CLASS; JOHN ordered more than one drink. The past few days had been both hectic and exciting. He fell asleep for an hour. When he awoke, he took out a *Playboy* magazine that he had purchased at the airport. After perusing it for a while, he decided to read the book about doing business in Thailand. By the time he'd read 20 pages, he wanted to go back to the United States.

The book described Thailand as a country that is 96% Buddhist and 4% Christian and Muslim. It said that you had to bow and say *Sawatdee-kah* when meeting someone. You had to place your hands together as though you were praying and hold them in a higher position if it were an elder or an important person and lower for a junior person. The Thais addressed you as *Khun* followed by your first name. Then John came to the part that said you could be arrested for bringing a *Playboy* magazine into the country. Wonderful; his timing was great! He made a mental note: toss magazine before getting off the plane. Wondering what he had gotten himself into, John ordered another drink and thought, "Whatever it is, I can do it!"

The pilot had to adjust his course due to some storms, so the plane arrived in Tokyo much later than its scheduled time. The connecting flight had already left. The airline decided to send the passengers to Hong Kong and then on to Bangkok. John had never been to Tokyo, Hong Kong or Bangkok, so each of these events was new and exciting.

As he was heading to the gate, a woman came up to him and said, "We are the only Americans on the flight. Have you done this before?" When he told her that it was his first trip to Asia, she replied, "What good are you?" and stormed away. John thought, "What a wench!"

The plane arrived in Hong Kong around midnight. The woman approached John again, but this time her demeanor was different. She apologized for her behavior and said that she was from South Carolina. She said she had never traveled to Asia and was going there to meet her fiancé, a Saudi prince, who was going to show her all around Thailand before they returned to the states for their wedding. John had many thoughts at this point. Was she telling him the truth? Was she a wacko? Was she really the innocent Southern girl that she seemed to be, standing in front of him with the vulnerability of a daughter?

He decided it was the latter and told her that he was going to arrange a hotel, determine the time and gate of their flight, and get some rest. He offered her the chance to tag along, and he would look after her. His new friend's name was Jackie. He managed to find a person who spoke some English and was able to help him with his tasks. Jackie was grateful for his help, and they agreed to meet at 7 a.m. for breakfast. It was difficult to sleep, because of course John's body was in a different time zone. Despite arranging a wake-up call, he was afraid he might oversleep. He was in a strange bed in a strange place.

Somehow both Americans managed to get a few hours of sleep. At breakfast they laughed about the previous day's adventure. They were in good spirits until they got into the cab to go to the airport. The cab driver asked where they were going and, upon hearing Bangkok, said, "It is a good thing you are going to Thailand!" When John asked why, he told them to look out the right side of the cab. He said, "There is a typhoon coming, but not in the direction of Thailand." Half the visible sky was very black and threatening. The other half was clear and sunny. However, Jackie was now visibly agitated again. John tried to calm her and said they were going to be okay. It was clear that she was scared. So was John, but he dared not show it.

When they got to the airport and found their gate, Jackie seemed to calm down. They could not arrange seats together. John gave Jackie his contact information for the Hilton in Bangkok in case they got separated at the airport. She wasn't sure her fiancé would know she was on the flight, but John reassured her.

Little did he know that giving her his contact information was going to be useful. The Bangkok airport was so crowded that John had a difficult time getting to the baggage claim. Jackie was not in sight, and John looked for her for a while before departing for the Hilton. He was very curious about what the country would be like.

CHAPTER 21

Doing Business in Thailand

JOHN ARRIVED AT THE HILTON WEARY FROM 22 hours of flying and the exhaustion of not having slept. As soon as he got to his room, he climbed into bed to get some sleep. That lasted about 10 minutes. The leader of the AT&T team, Steve Jones, called John's room. AT&T would be competing with the Japanese, the Canadians and every other country that wanted to bid on the tender offer from the Telephone Organization of Thailand (TOT).

Steve and John had never met. Steve wanted John to join him for some fun in Pat Pong, which was, and still is, the entertainment district of the city and perhaps of the world.

Drinking was the very last thing John wanted to do. He tried to say no, but Steve wasn't having it. They were going.

John soon learned that the reason you couldn't bring a *Playboy* magazine into Thailand was that it competed with their pornography. Even in John's wildest imagination, he would not have come up with a place as lascivious as Pat Pong. Women lured tourists into bars with smiles, laughter and gestures.

John was amazed at the crowds and the craziness. When you crossed a street, you took your life into your hands. You had better not get caught in the middle of the street when the light changed. It was like the Indianapolis 500. The cars, cabs and *tuktuks* were noisy with horns blowing, bells ringing and motors racing. When John and Steve came to a strange-looking structure in the street, John asked what it was. It looked like a wall in the shape of a wide V. But there was nothing inside. It wasn't for a payphone. It wasn't an advertising structure. It didn't have a seat for a bus stop. Steve said it was a place where you could urinate. There was no plumbing, and John was in disbelief.

Steve took John to what appeared to be a bar. John was dazed and was therefore not very observant.

They were sipping beers when Steve asked John if he had ever had a body massage. John said that he had not, but he knew of them. Steve explained that in Thailand the term "body massage" meant something different. It meant that they massage your body with theirs. John said, "What?" Steve laughed. He said that John would find that so many things in Thailand were different and affordable. He said a body massage would cost the equivalent of $20 and would come with a bath. Steve told John to turn around, and when he did, he saw a large window. Behind the window were at least 50 women. Each had a number. Steve explained that patrons would pick a number, but John preferred to head back to the hotel and get some much-needed sleep.

He slept like a log that night. The next morning, he received a phone call from Jackie and her fiancé. Sure enough, he was a Saudi prince. He thanked John for looking after her and invited him to tour the palaces of Bangkok later in the week. John accepted and had a lovely time. They even visited the grand palace where the king and queen lived. For years afterward,

John received a Christmas card from Jackie and her prince, until at some point they lost touch. He learned that they did subsequently marry and live in the United States.

John worked with the AT&T team for five weeks, and he created the financial plan and the training plan. Each of the consultants had a gigantic room with a nice-sized desk and a chair. At that time, the Thai hotels were ranked among the top in the world. The first time John had lunch and finished a drink, another was put in front of him. When he used a pat of butter, another replaced it instantly. When he put out a cigarette, a clean ashtray was placed before him. If he needed his clothes laundered, they came back cleaned, pressed and neatly folded in record time. John was not accustomed to this kind of treatment and to the fantastic value of the U.S. dollar.

The consultants worked separately most of the time, but Steve brought them together for planning and coordination meetings. During this period John met a man named Paul Drew, the proposal writer for AT&T. Paul was also from New Jersey, and he and John became friends. They hung out together and explored different restaurants. During one of the dinners, John learned of an amazing coincidence—Paul had been his assistant Debbie's English teacher in Fair Haven, New Jersey. Here he had traveled halfway around the world to meet someone who had taught his assistant. The world had just become much smaller!

Each day after work, the AT&T team would meet for a drink in the Hilton lounge. At their first gathering, John was sitting on a couch talking with Steve when a woman dressed in a full-length, gold, sequined gown came over and knelt next to him. He quietly whispered to Steve, "What is she doing?"

Steve replied, "She wants to take your drink order." John asked why she was kneeling, and Steve said that's just what they do.

John couldn't imagine an American woman kneeling in a gown to take his drink order. Her name was La Kanika, and she was the hostess. She worked with another lovely young woman named Summa Lee. Each day, the women would serve their drinks and converse with them about the day. They were charming, outgoing and very optimistic. Once when John and Steve said they had been to Pat Pong, she giggled and said, "Khun John, you have to be careful in Pat Pong. You mustn't be a bad boy." She was so charmingly cute and yet so formal in dress and manner.

There was a certain innocence about La Kanika and Summa Lee that was such a contrast to the women in Pat Pong that one day John asked La Kanika how there could be such a difference in the way women conducted themselves. She explained that there were two classes in Thailand. The upper-class women were not even permitted to hold hands with their fiancés in public. The lower-class women were permitted to do whatever they chose to earn a living for themselves and their families. She explained that the country had no welfare or unemployment insurance and that being resourceful in caring for your family was regarded as honorable. It was quite a learning experience.

During one of the weekend breaks, John and Paul decided to take a boat ride on the Chao Phraya River. The ride took them past shacks that were built on docks that provided access to boats on the river. They were made of tin and had what appeared to be burlap curtains that opened in the front to allow access to potential customers on the river.

This was an active commercial district, though the only access was by boat. Everything was sold here, from produce to clothing to artifacts. As they cruised down the river, they passed incredible poverty, sometimes followed by a statue of Buddha made entirely of gold. There was great wealth coexisting with extreme poverty. They also saw women washing clothes in the river and kids swimming. This was a shock to them; the water was so dirty that they didn't want to be splashed for fear of disease. They saw both a dead dog and a dead rat float by. John was wishing his kids could have been there to see the poverty firsthand and to appreciate all the wonderful benefits they had living in the United States.

John called Pat and his children every week. To place a phone call to the states was quite the ordeal. You had to schedule it with the operator hours in advance. Sometimes she would place it at the agreed-upon time and sometimes she wouldn't. The time difference of 12 hours made it even more complicated. John learned that Ross Sheer had sent the retainer check. Also, John's consultants were working on establishing a pricing matrix for National Pay Telephone's services so that a tariff could be filed. Both were comfortable doing the work.

While the business side seemed to be going reasonably well, Pat was really sad. During their marriage Pat and John had never been apart this long, and John was feeling her pain every time they spoke. He knew that what he was doing was necessary, and that it would soon be over. He was hopeful that the investment of time and effort would be worth it. On his side of the phone, there were private tears at the end of each call that would never be revealed.

Interestingly, Bell Canada representatives were also staying at the Hilton and, in fact, also had drinks in the lounge every night. After a week or so, the groups decided to mingle, but with a strict rule in place: no work discussions, as they were both competing for the same business.

When Bell Canada's team leader heard that John would be going to Tokyo, he shared a story from his last visit there. Late one night, there was a knock on his door. He opened it to find a young Japanese woman holding a sign that said "compliments of" the company he was visiting. He thanked her and said he was married, and he had to decline the offer. Fifteen minutes later, there was another knock at the door. This time there was a young Japanese man holding the same sign. Everyone laughed. He said they also had private clubs where businessmen took their clients.

During his time in Thailand, John went out in the field with the technical team. One day he discovered telephone pole lines that were located in canals. John was wondering how they would address this, since he didn't recall seeing pole lines in canals in New Jersey. U.S. pole lines were usually running down streets or in some cases located behind row houses in cities. This city was full of crisscrossed telephone lines that presented a less than aesthetic view of the sky. The operating environment was very different. At the time, it took longer than a year to get a telephone line installed in your residence.

Toward the project's end, John wanted to take a trip to Pattaya Beach because a friend had raved about it. He asked Ray, one of the Bell Canada consultants, to join him. During their morning bus ride to the beach, they were offered beer and liquor. Ray opted for a beer, and John joined him, although he was not accustomed to drinking in the morning.

Shortly thereafter, a man on the bus approached them with a brochure. He showed them pictures of a beautiful island with bikini-clad women and said it was where Europeans vacationed. The idea was appealing to them, so they agreed to go. When they arrived at the beach, they raced to their hotel, dropped off their bags and went back to the dock to catch the boat to the island.

They continued drinking beer on the boat. Along the way, in a bit of foreshadowing, John noticed the huge rocks that protruded up from the South China Sea, and he was thinking any captain would have to navigate very carefully around them. When the boat reached the island, John and Ray knew that they had been had. All they saw were emaciated dogs and bars. People were selling T-shirts and other wares in which they had no interest. There were no European women.

Since they had to spend the day there and were already into their cups, Ray's suggestion that they make a pledge to hit every bar sounded like a swell idea. Clearly, they were not in a position to make sound decisions.

A bit later, they were walking near the beach when the captain of the boat started screaming at them. They had no idea what he was saying or why he was yelling at them. When he realized they didn't understand him, he pointed to the sky and said, "Typhoon!" John looked up and saw fast-moving black clouds, the likes of which he had never seen. The captain motioned them back to the boat, so they got on.

Within 10 minutes, they were in the middle of the sea engulfed in a major storm without any visibility. The boat was rocking from port to starboard and from bow to stern. The Thai people were clutching their seats and clenching their teeth. Fear was evident on all their faces. Ray and John were at the bar, and John couldn't believe how they had allowed themselves to get into this situation. Then Ray said something John would never forget. He said, "John, if we are going to check out, let's have another beer," and that is exactly what they did.

It occurred to John that dying was a distinct possibility. The majestic and unforgiving rocks they had passed on the way there permeated his thoughts. The captain was now in complete control of their lives. John hoped he had navigation gear that would avoid the rocks and keep them on a steady and safe course. It occurred to him that if he died there, no one would ever know what happened. He hadn't told anyone where he was going. Even if they found out that he had gone to Pattaya Beach, it would have been difficult to trace his steps to a boat that had gone down in the sea.

After what seemed like an eternity, the sky began clearing and the ocean was visible. They made it back safely, and John kissed the ground when they got to shore. He was impressed with the captain's skills.

As they were walking back to the resort, a little girl came up to John and asked him to buy flowers. John had just thrown flowers away that he had bought from a little boy. When he said no, she started screaming and jumped up and attached herself to him. John gave her five dollars so she would get off him and go away; he did not want to survive a typhoon only to end up in jail in a strange country. Ray thought it was hysterical, but John was not amused. Both were happy to make it back to Bangkok intact.

When it was time for John to leave Bangkok, it was time to call Mr. Motsumoto, as Mr. Wasumi had suggested. The conversation wasn't exactly smooth:

"Hello!"

"Hello, may I speak with Mr. Motsumoto, please?"

A stern voice replied, "This is Motsumoto."

"Mr. Motsumoto, this is Mr. Gammino."

"Who?" (It sounded like "Whooo.")

"Mr. Gammino."

"*Who?*"

"Mr. Gammino."

"*WHO?*"

John could feel his blood pressure rising. "Mr. Motsumoto, do you know Mr. Wasumi?"

"Oh yes, Wasumi big boss!"

"Mr. Wasumi told me to contact you. I am working in Bangkok, but my work is coming to a close, and Mr. Wasumi wanted you to arrange for me to visit your plants in Tokyo."

"Mr. Gammino, I will get back to you. Where are you staying, and what is your room number?"

Two days later, John received a message at the Hilton. It said: "Mr. Gammino, take a taxi to airport. You take this flight to Narita Airport in Tokyo." John smiled as he read the details that were provided, and then he read the rest of the message. "When you get to the airport, you take the limo to Daiichi Terminal. When you get to Daiichi Terminal, you take a cab to Daiichi Hotel. When you reach the hotel, you call this number for Mr. Asada. Mr. Asada will take you on a tour of our plants and make other arrangements."

As soon as he returned to his room, Mr. Motsumoto called. He asked if John had received his message. John said that he had. He asked John to read it back to him. John did. He asked if John understood his message. John said that he did. Then he said, "Mr. Gammino, next time you are in Thailand, I would like to meet you. Please say hi to my friends in Tokyo."

John knew his next challenge was about to begin — speaking to Japanese engineers about fiber optics. "Oh God!" he wondered, "Where is that cocktail napkin?"

CHAPTER 22

Doing Business in Japan

JOHN FINISHED HIS WORK IN BANGKOK A FEW days early. This made him happy because he was anxious to see Pat and the kids, and also to get started on the contract with National Pay Telephone.

His trip to Tokyo was uneventful, and he arranged to have breakfast with Mr. Asada at his hotel. John was wondering how Mr. Asada would recognize him, but then he smiled to himself. It would be the same way that he recognized Mr. Wasumi at the restaurant in New Jersey. He was likely to be the only American in the place. Sure enough, Mr. Asada emerged from the many other faces in the lobby and approached John saying, "Mr. Gammino?" John was pleasantly surprised to learn that Mr. Asada had spent considerable time in New York and spoke fluent English.

After breakfast, they took a train to one of the company's plants. John met engineers and managers and toured offices and manufacturing facilities. Questions were directed at him from all angles. The Tim Schilling napkin training kicked in. John had memorized everything on the napkin. He was engaged in discussions that covered very technical matters. He held his ground with his counterparts. Between the RJA guidance and Tim's training, no one could tell how much he didn't know. At one point he was asked, "Mr. Gammino, are you an engineer?" John said he was not, but that he had spent his career in the management of technology.

John's Japanese host took him to dinner at a restaurant that had hosted U.S. presidents. John was amazed that they knew he drank Scotch and put a fresh bottle of Dewar's on the table next to him. He was enjoying the experience until he was served something on a skewer that didn't taste very good. He asked Mr. Asada what they were eating. When he replied, "chicken hearts," John thought he was going to be sick. He dutifully ate it so as not to insult his host. He then said that he was full and couldn't eat another thing.

Mr. Asada then took John around Tokyo to show him the sights. Tokyo is a bustling city with lights and sounds that rival those of New York. Mr. Asada was a gracious host, but he kept trying to get market information out of John. John told him many times that he would provide all the answers to his questions when Mr. Wasumi had signed the consulting agreement. They toured Tokyo in the cleanest cab that John had ever seen. The driver wore white gloves. The seats were lined in white linen. John remarked to Mr. Asada that cabs in Tokyo were not the same as those in New York. He laughed. He told John that Japanese people are very clean and love their cars. He mused that when people park in New York, it is not uncommon to bump into the car in back or in front of you. He said, "In Tokyo, that is a fight." He said most Japanese men wash and wax their cars every weekend.

When the hour got to be late, John thought Mr. Asada would drop him off at the hotel, but he should have known better (especially given the story he had heard from the Bell Canada rep). Instead, they headed for a private club. When they arrived upstairs, there was a nicely decorated room with a piano, and not a soul was there.

John excused himself to go to the restroom. When he returned, there were several women in the room. One was playing the piano. Another bottle of Scotch was in front of him. He was shown to a seat between two Japanese women. Mr. Asada and his friends were drinking and laughing. They had removed their jackets. John did the same. It was a hot summer day, and he was wearing a short-sleeved dress shirt. The women on either side of him were playing with the hair on his arms. Mr. Asada informed John that they were not accustomed to seeing hair on men's arms, since Japanese men are most often without arm hair. They laughed, drank and sang.

As the hour approached 1 a.m., John was wondering what would happen next. Mr. Asada abruptly said, "Okay, we go." He secured a cab and dropped John off at his hotel. John was amazed that the evening was ending so abruptly. Mr. Asada said they would return there on John's next trip. Then he figured it out: He wasn't providing enough market information for them to proceed any further.

CHAPTER 23

A Happy Homecoming

THE VISIT TO TOKYO ENDED AFTER THREE DAYS, and John boarded a flight to Kennedy Airport. When he arrived, he was shocked at how poorly customs agents treated foreign visitors. The agents were yelling at the newcomers because they didn't understand the instructions on the signs and were not following directions. John had traveled halfway around the world and hadn't seen anything like this. People often tried to help him even though they didn't speak the same language. He was appalled at how these visitors were experiencing America, perhaps for the first time.

The flight from Tokyo to New York was more than 13 hours long, and John was utterly exhausted when he got home. But he was delighted to see Pat and the kids and to feel the love that comes with rejoining family after an extended absence. Pat told him she couldn't stop crying when he was away. She said people would ask if she had heard from John, and she would start crying. They would ask her if she knew what he was doing in Thailand, and she would say it didn't matter, just so he was back in bed with her when he got home. True to form, the Gamminos acted like newlyweds the whole next week.

After a weekend break at home, John returned to his new office to check on the status of the work for National Pay Telephone. His colleagues had done some fine work in laying out a competitive rate structure, and John paid them both well for their efforts. He would now work on constructing a tariff that the company could file with regulatory commissions in the states where they were seeking permission to operate.

John never did sign a contract with Nissho Iwai. He met with Mr. Wasumi and his staff, but the two sides just could not come to terms. John was always grateful for the opportunity to have met them and to have seen their operations in Japan.

The National Pay Telephone contract became the launching pad for the new JRA consulting business. Working with NPT was not only lucrative; it also generated new business. John represented the company in regulatory hearings before the Illinois Commerce Commission; NPT had to appear before the commission to get approval to enter the market for pay telephone services. During the hearing, 10 attorneys representing the local exchange carriers in the state questioned John. The hearings went well, and John's testimony held up strongly against the barrage of questions. NPT was approved to do business in Illinois. JRA was a real company, and John had succeeded in making it so. He had taken a big chance in leaving New Jersey Bell, but it appeared that he was now on a successful new career path.

A few years into this new endeavor, a letter arrived from Lisa. She apologized for coming into their lives and abruptly leaving. She told Pat and John that they had a new grandson named Nicholas. She said her pregnancy and delivery gave her a new sense of understanding of life and the decisions that were made when she was born. She wanted to reconnect with Pat and John and her brother and sisters. Pat was still upset that Lisa had hurt the kids when she had come into their lives and then suddenly left. John smiled, for he'd known Lisa would one day come back and that Pat would forgive her when she did. John picked up the phone and called Lisa, and they had a wonderful conversation. Afterward, John handed the phone to Pat, and within minutes she was laughing and talking happily with her eldest daughter. The phone call lasted a long time. Lisa said she was a flight attendant for People Express and that she would visit the family in the coming weeks.

From that day on, Lisa and Pat talked regularly on the phone. Over the years Lisa, her husband, Charlie, and her children, Nicholas and Katie, would visit Pat and John. Once, when John and Pat went to visit Lisa and Charlie in Hamburg, New York, they met Vic and Neva, who had been so kind to Pat when she was a lonely, pregnant teenager. The couple lived in Attica, a town not far from Lisa's home. It took some doing to find them, but they were glad they did because they all had a wonderful time.

Pat, John and Lisa became very close over the years. Pat and John would often reflect that they now had known Lisa for more years than they hadn't known her. She turned out to be an amazing woman. They were very proud of her and very happy grandparents of her lovely children.

Lisa would later tell John about her feelings on that first trip to Lincroft to meet her brother and sisters. She said she felt so comfortable and loved. She explained that she'd just wanted to crawl into one of the kids' beds and stay there in the warmth of her newly discovered family. But she knew that wasn't something she could make happen. She said that when she had told her adoptive mother about Pat and John, her mother had heaped guilt on her unmercifully. She felt badly that she had interrupted their lives, disappeared, and now had

More than 25 years after Neva and Vic befriended Pat while she was pregnant, they were reunited with Pat and Lisa and they also got to meet John.

Lisa celebrates her daughter Katie's graduation from the Summit Academy with her husband Charlie and their son Nicholas.

no right to intrude again. It took her a long time to overcome this view. Eventually, she realized it was important to get back in touch with the family who had instantly welcomed her.

Pat was making some realizations, too. As Lisa recognized her desire to reunite with her family, Pat recognized new desires within herself—and began developing into a new woman.

CHAPTER 24

Who is This Woman?

MEANWHILE, MAUREEN WAS 20 YEARS OLD and in college at Old Dominion University in Virginia. Melissa was 17 and Mike was 12. Both lived at home in Lincroft. John was busy with his consulting practice, which had become very demanding and successful. Pat had become a teacher's assistant with the Lincroft School, working with special needs children.

One day, Pat announced to the family that she was going to head a fund-raising drive for a young man who had brain cancer. A neighbor had asked her if she would do it, and to John's surprise, Pat agreed. She organized sporting and social events and raised $10,000 for the family.

As she was becoming well known in her new role, Pat began exuding different aspects of her persona that were unfamiliar to John. It was a period when recycling had become a new priority around the country. Pat wanted to patent an invention she'd created that she called "Saddle Bags." She envisioned a trash can with two side bins, one for glass and cans and one for paper products. The flexibility of her idea would allow for any combination of recyclable products in the extra bins.

John arranged a meeting with a patent attorney, and the attorney told Pat that pursuing a patent could be very expensive. He suggested that Pat call Rubbermaid and pitch her idea to them. She should tell them she would reveal her idea if Rubbermaid agreed to pay her a percentage of the profits if they chose to use the idea. Pat accepted that answer.

John didn't hear anything else about it until he was having coffee one morning and the phone rang. A vice president of Rubbermaid was calling for Pat. John couldn't really hear the conversation, but he did hear Pat say, "Okay, then I will meet you in the marketplace." John could not believe it—Pat never made statements like that. Nor did she ever call vice presidents of corporations.

John began to wonder if Pat had latent talent and abilities that had been hidden during the child-rearing years. He could not fathom her new lexicon and the aggressive leadership role she was exhibiting. He saw many new aspects of Pat's personality. She had already been known in the community for her deep commitment to caring about friends and neighbors, and she was loved by all who knew her. Now her abilities seemed to be expanding geometrically; she had organized numerous benefit events.

While her new talents were emerging, something else was happening to Pat. The hurt that she'd managed to bury from her experience in Attica was coming out for the first time. It came out of her with the fury of a bad storm. She told John it was time for her to have a discussion with his parents, Rose and Jake. She was going to drive more than an hour to their house and tell them about the pain she had carried all these years. John did not deter her; he knew it was important for her to release the hurt. He offered to go with her, but she wanted to go alone.

John's parents, Jake and Rose, celebrated their 65th wedding anniversary in 2007.

When Pat left for Phillipsburg, John called his parents with some advice. He recommended that they mostly listen to her and not really talk unless they were answering her questions. He also suggested that they shouldn't push back on anything she said. "She just has to get some things off her chest, and the best way through this is to let her say what she needs to say."

The conversation went as John had predicted. All the hurt Pat had buried for years came out with passion. When it was over, Rose, Jake and Pat entered into a new understanding that allowed them to become closer over the years.

John was impressed with Pat's new persona and the assertiveness she was exhibiting in her own life and in the community. He was in awe of her range of capabilities. The 44-year-old woman he had known since age 12 was evolving into a more vivacious and energetic leader in the community. He was very proud of her. As Pat thrived with new initiatives, John couldn't have predicted the next devastating blow — and the pivot away from his business.

CHAPTER 25

Business on Fire

JOHN HAD DONE SO WELL WITH HIS CONSULTING business that he gained international recognition. He was invited to speak at national and international conferences. He was quoted in major newspapers and magazines around the world. His colleagues would joke that he had gained this notoriety from his 1,000-square-foot office in a small town in New Jersey, but that is exactly what happened. John had turned what seemed like a major risk into a highly successful endeavor.

On the heels of this success, he decided to purchase a business condominium in Hazlet, New Jersey. It was a sound business decision because he owned the condominium personally, and his business paid rent to him instead of to someone else.

Maureen, Melissa and Michael were now out of college and were all doing well. Maureen went to work for John after a major bout with chronic fatigue syndrome took her out of her successful sales role with Russ Berrie. Melissa was a successful mother; she and her husband Bill had a beautiful son

Maureen always loved the company of her grandmother Rose.

Bill and Melissa enjoy relaxing at the Gamminos' house.

Kim and Mike were happy to stop by for a visit.

and daughter. Mike was married to Kim and was working with a major pharmaceutical company as a sales representative.

On a warm July night of that same year, Maureen and Pat were sitting in the kitchen chatting. Around midnight, ADT called to say that a burglar alarm was ringing at John's office, but they thought it might be a false alarm. The ADT rep said she was dispatching the police just in case. Pat and Maureen decided not to awaken John.

Then ADT called back and said they didn't think it was a false alarm. Pat woke John up, and he and Maureen headed for the office. On the way, John called the police so that he and Maureen wouldn't be mistaken for burglars. When he reached the police, the dispatcher said that it was not a robbery but a fire, and a bad one at that. John's heart raced, and then he heard sirens. He lowered the window, and even though they were a mile away, they could smell the smoke. He said, "This must be a terrible fire."

When they arrived at the office, there were fire trucks all around. Police had cordoned off the area, but they let John and Maureen through when he identified himself as the owner. The flames were shooting into the air uncontrollably, and the roof of the building had collapsed. Maureen put her arms around John to comfort him, but it didn't help. He knew he was about to lose everything, and he was in a state of shock. Maureen was worried he would faint, so she held onto his arm. When the fire was finally out and only smoldering embers remained, John took one last look at the roofless structure with partial walls and departed with Maureen for home.

No one got much sleep that night. Pat tried to console him, but John was devastated. The next day, he called the insurance company and learned that his representative would be delayed in getting to the site. At the same time, John learned that the building inspector for the town was going to have the walls knocked down. He said they were a hazard to the area and could easily tip over with a very heavy wind. John was upset with him for not caring that the insurance rep was on his way. John went to the site with his still camera and his video camera and took plenty of images.

As if the devastation wasn't bad enough, John soon received a visit from the Monmouth County Arson Squad. They told him the cause of the fire was arson, and it became clear to John that he was their prime suspect. The detectives questioned him and learned that he had lost everything.

John was both sick and incredulous. Who could have done this? He and his family went over possibilities. He couldn't imagine that anyone could have hated him to the extent of deliberately burning down his office building. He had sent the burnt computers and disks to a lab in California to see if any

The office building on the day after the fire.

of the files could be saved, but they could not. To make matters worse, John had hired a backup company that had come to his office and copied his 1,000 most important documents. Two copies of the backup disk were produced. One was kept in the office and the other at home. However, one day John had inadvertently taken the second copy to the office. Both were burned in the fire. He called the company that had produced the disks, but because of their privacy policy, they had destroyed the media they had produced for John.

The insurance money he would receive might cover reconstruction of the office, but not much more. The loss was calculated as the depreciated value of the furniture and computers and the price of blank disks. The real value of John's business, however, was the information contained in his files. Needless to say, the insurance coverage was a major disappointment. The arson squad realized there had been no motive for John to set his own office on fire. They did question other business associates with whom John had had disagreements, but they found no one to charge with the crime of arson.

Maureen told John that she was going to get him back in business, and she did just that. The fire had occurred on a Thursday. Maureen leased space the very next day from an office-sharing firm located in Red Bank, New Jersey. On Monday morning, JRA was back in business. She called each major client and told them about the fire. Each offered to send the last two years' worth of files so JRA could rebuild its client documentation. Maureen had risen to a new position in JRA and was destined to become an integral part of the business management team.

John was still reeling from the effects of the fire when George Giardelli came to visit him. George and John had worked together on projects with the Port Authority. George's firm had actually subcontracted work to JRA. However, George's company was looking to cut staff, so George approached John about working for him. John told him he would route work to George when it was available, but that George should think about buying John's business. George was 10 years younger, and John thought he might like the idea of owning his own business. John had just signed multiyear contracts with his largest federal and state government clients. George took John's offer and ran with it. He found a financing organization that would back the purchase.

George and John agreed on a three-year payout arrangement. John would subcontract with George for the three years. On December 31, 2000, George would own JRA outright. At that point, John would begin the process of thinking about his next steps in the business world.

CHAPTER 26

Welcome to Vero Beach

JOHN HATED NEW JERSEY'S COLD WEATHER AND always talked about going to a warmer climate. One year, New Jersey had 12 snowstorms between December and February. Bill and Rosemary Clancey had invited Pat and John to Vero Beach, Florida, many times. John finally said to Pat, "I think it is time to take our friends up on their invitation." The Gamminos traveled to Florida in 1996 to stay with the Clanceys.

The Los Angeles Dodgers' spring training camp was in Vero Beach, so Bill took John to a baseball game. John was so quiet that Bill asked if he was uncomfortable and wanted to leave. John laughed and told Bill that he was in heaven. He was taking in the sun and the game and was in a happy trance.

As Pat and John became more familiar with Vero Beach, they fell in love with it. Many of John's older friends from New Jersey Bell had retired there. Pat and John agreed they would try to rent a place in Vero Beach the following winter. John would test whether he could manage his consulting business from a virtual location, because technology was making virtual management a real possibility.

The Gamminos did rent a condominium in Vero Beach that winter, a double unit in fact. Maureen came along for the winter and Melissa and Mike visited when they could. The place was so large that the girls could Rollerblade through it with ease. It faced the Atlantic Ocean and had a beautiful deck. It was decorated in an Asian motif, and it had its own Jacuzzi room with mirrors all around. The master bedroom was lined with mirrors too, and there was a step up to the king-size bed. Pat and John loved it, although Pat said it reminded her of a house of prostitution.

While John was engaged in the JRA business with George, Pat and Maureen were getting comfortable in the condo they had rented in Vero Beach. John contacted a local office supply store and rented a desk, a chair and a fax machine. He also had a telephone line installed in the home office. John would work during the day while Pat and Maureen enjoyed the sunshine and the beach.

That winter John learned that he could manage his business remotely, and so they rented condos in Vero Beach for the next two winters. In 1999, Pat was on a house tour, and she mentioned to her friend that she had an appointment to see a condo in Grand Harbor the next day. The woman in front of Pat turned and said, "I could not help but overhear your conversation. My husband and I live in Grand Harbor and were planning to list our condo for sale, but we haven't yet. Would you like to see it?" Having looked at plenty of condos in various communities, Pat jumped at the idea, and an appointment was set for the next day.

When John and Pat walked into the condo, they both immediately knew it was the one. The couple that owned it were Bernie and Kathy Lavins. Pat and John told them that they were very interested in purchasing the condo. Kathy and Pat were hugging each other, and John was thinking, *Geez, Pat, would you stop this? I have to negotiate a price with the guy.*

The sale was made, and John and Pat became residents and also members of the Grand Harbor Golf and Beach Club. They absolutely loved the place. Their condo was located on the harbor and had a spectacular view of the sailboats and other vessels moored there. There were dolphins, manatee, pelicans and other wildlife that made every day interesting. They were happy there for two winter seasons.

A friend of the Gamminos was also interested in moving to Grand Harbor, so Pat contacted a real estate agent about seeing some homes. Pat came back and told John she had seen a house for sale that she loved. John said, "We don't need a house. This condo is beautiful."

Pat replied, "We need more room when the kids come to visit. You're going to love this house. It's right on the golf course and it has a pool."

It took some doing, but Pat convinced John to look at the property. John did not want to move. He told Pat he would make one bid for the property, and if the guy said no, that was it. Pat agreed. John made what he thought was a low bid, but the owner of the house took it. John was amazed. The owner eventually told him that he had just made a good bit of money selling his company. He was building a 10,000 square-foot-home in Maryland, and all he wanted was to get his money out of the house. Therefore, he took the low bid.

Now that they owned two houses and a condo, John decided to sell the house in Lincroft and the condo in Vero Beach. He wanted to downsize in New Jersey to a condo and have their main residence in Vero Beach. While searching for a condo in New Jersey, Pat and John came upon a community in Neptune,

New Jersey, that was just being built. They purchased a house in preconstruction mode that would be finished within the year. John was sure they were going to own four homes or none.

They put the Lincroft house on the market without an agent. John devised an ad that he was certain would attract buyers. It was placed in the local papers on Thursday, and it invited prospective buyers to a showing on Saturday by appointment. The ad was a success, and the people from the first appointment bought the house. The woman with the second appointment actually arrived at the house early and wanted a chance to outbid the people from the first appointment. But Pat fell in love with the two children from the first appointment and wanted them to have the house.

John told her that she was making an emotional decision and that selling the house was a business matter that required objectivity to get the best price. It was no use. Pat prevailed and John, as he did most often, gave in to whatever would make Pat happy. While the Lincroft house was under contract, the condo in Grand Harbor was sold. John was seriously happy about the seamless transition from New Jersey to Florida.

Over the following year, Pat worked on furnishing their new residence in Florida. She was exceptionally good at decorating and loved to shop for home goods. John, on the other hand, was anxious to get the house furnished as quickly as possible. Pat took her time, though, and in the end John complimented her on her hard work and great taste.

Grand Harbor turned out to be Pat and John's slice of paradise. They made many friends and their social lives were extremely active. Pat took up golf and with her friends founded a group called the "Oniners." The name came from a prominent letter from the last name of each member of the group. The group included Pat, Marge Randazzo, Jan Oneidas, Catherine O'Donnell and others. Catherine put a set of rules together for the Oniners that put John in hysterics. It seemed the group was all about lunch, and maybe a golf game would break out. They had rules like "If you don't like the way your ball lies, move it" or "If you don't feel like finishing the hole, put the ball in your pocket." All the rules were in the spirit of having fun and not being encumbered by the way their men played golf. Pat would always laugh at John when he picked up some loose grass and let it go to find out which way the wind was blowing. She'd say, "What difference does it make?" John would shake his head. It mattered to him, but it wasn't worth arguing in paradise.

CHAPTER 27

Life is Good

IN 2001, JOHN AND TWO FRIENDS FORMED A GOLF group that played on Tuesdays and Thursdays. John agreed to be the commissioner of the group. It was initially known as TTG (Tuesday/Thursday Group). The acceptance of players into the group was based on two primary criteria. First, the player had to be a good guy that others would enjoy being around. Second, regardless of handicap, the player had to play at a pace that would not slow down his foursome or others behind his foursome.

John also arranged to have two parties for the players and their wives. One was in January when everyone was there, including the snowbirds. The second was in the first week of May to recognize the close of the formal season. The group was tightly knit—the golfers had formed a bond over their sport, but the wives also became good friends. This resulted in several of the couples buying homes in Grand Harbor. At its peak, there were 37 players in the group.

Tom Lauda was a member of the golf group. Tom and his wife, also named Pat, were very close friends of the Gamminos.

Pat and John enjoyed a Dancing with the Stars fundraiser in Vero Beach.

As the couples' relationship was growing, their children, Kim and Mike, began dating. The relationship was great for both the parents and the kids, and eventually Kim and Mike got married.

Tom and Pat and John and Pat would often go on weekend trips together. On one occasion, they were sitting in box seats at a Miami Dolphins game, and the Hooters girls were in the box next to them. Tom and Pat, who were both Leos, were always known to do pranks on each other. On this day, Tom was making some macho comments about his admiration of the Hooters girls. When Pat went to the ladies' room a while later, several Hooters girls were there. After explaining the situation, she playfully asked if the three girls would be kind enough to stop in at the box next to theirs to have a drink with Tom. They readily agreed. When the door opened and the Hooters girls walked in with Pat, Tom lost it. He couldn't believe his eyes. Pat had one-upped him; this was better than his last prank on her. That prank had involved a visit to a CVS store; Tom had put a package of extra-large condoms in Pat's basket without her knowledge. Pat was embarrassed and chagrined when the checker pulled out the condoms for scanning.

These two continually did things that were outlandish. On one occasion they were riding the 25-cent kiddie horses outside of a department store in Vero Beach. Many shoppers thought they were nuts, and one lady actually said so. The two of them were hysterical with laughter and the lady's comment fell on deaf ears.

Pat became very involved in the Vero Beach community. She worked with Habitat for Humanity. She worked with disadvantaged orchard workers. And she was the first one to support any friend who was in need. When their friends Marge and Rosemary had heart surgery, Pat was there for support, even if it meant staying in Florida while John was in New Jersey. When their friend Tom had heart surgery, she stayed with his wife throughout the critical period of his recovery. Pat became a very well-known and well-respected member of the community.

The Gamminos celebrate New Year's with a little karaoke.

The entire Gammino family loved coming to Grand Harbor and using the facilities of the resort community. There were two golf courses, a tennis club, a beach club on the ocean and a marina. John and Pat had so many social events that it seemed they were busy most nights of the week. John was able to balance his business obligations with his family and social life.

Pat and John stayed in Vero Beach nine months of the year and returned to New Jersey for the summers. Each year for 20 years, the entire family (four generations) gathered at Long Beach Island for a week. It was a very special time for the family, and it served to bring them close together in an atmosphere of fun and sun. Each year, Maureen would have a weekend with her niece and nephews to set the agenda for the week. Three nights were special entertainment nights; examples included a Hawaiian night, a '50s night, and a lip-synching contest. The kids would decide who had the duty of cooking breakfast and

Pat and John in full Hawaiian regalia for a dress-up night at their annual family vacation in Long Beach Island.

dinner for each night of the vacation. It was quite a feat to feed the crew and it required considerable planning.

Pat and John also went on special trips with friends over the years. Liz and Wayne Pesaresi were close friends from high school. Pat and John always stayed with them when they visited Phillipsburg. They also went on vacations together in later years. In 2015, John put a trip together for a visit to Tuscany and the Amalfi Coast. They flew to Rome and took a train to Pisa, where they were to begin their Italian vacation. Wayne volunteered to get the train tickets. When the train arrived, they got into the first-class cabin. Wayne and Liz had big suitcases and it was difficult getting through the narrow

Pat, with friend Liz Pesaresi on a train to Pisa, Italy, had to hide her laughter because the other occupants of the car were extremely annoyed at the Americans' large luggage.

corridor that led to the cabins. Two of the men who sat in their cabin did not have much room for their feet and were visibly annoyed at the big pieces of luggage that were consuming all the leg room. Pat had to cover her face with her coat because she was going to burst out laughing. Liz was trying hard to look away from Pat. Wayne couldn't see the girls' faces, but John did, and all three of them nearly lost it.

Pretty soon, the conductor came along and asked to see their tickets. When Wayne handed them over, she said they were not supposed to be in first class. They had to move into the narrow hall again and walk several cars back to find a seat in coach. Wayne was sure he had purchased first-class

Pat and John loved spending time with their grandchildren. From left: Trey Gammino, Chandler Reeson, Ella Gammino, Ryan Reeson, Samuel Reeson, and Christopher Henderson.

tickets, but he hadn't. They were chagrined at having to leave their first-class seats, but they laughed until they reached another car that had room for them and their suitcases.

When they arrived in Pisa, they went to the rental car agency and were surprised to find a super-friendly staff that provided them with a station wagon with an automatic transmission and plenty of room for their luggage. The proprietor said that if they did not want to return the car, they could just call him, and he would arrange to have it picked up. He could not have been nicer. The couples visited many places in Tuscany. They used their condo in Terricciola as their base and ventured to a new village every day. Lucca, Siena,

Picciola and San Gimignano were among them. They were having a great time. They visited a castle and enjoyed wine and lunch at a local winery. They hired two local cooks to prepare meals on several nights. One cook spoke no English; the other did and assisted with pouring wine and serving dinner. The food was outrageously good. The cooks and the four Americans got along very well, and much laughter accompanied each dinner.

At one of the late evening dinners, they ran out of wine. One of the cooks had a friend who owned a local winery. The two cooks and Wayne and John drove to the winery, and the woman who answered the door said her husband was in bed, but she would wake him. Wayne and John thought it might turn into a very bad scene. However, the man was very gracious and welcoming. He was happy to sell them a few bottles of his wine. The Italian hospitality and friendliness were overwhelming at times.

Wayne and John had studied Italian using the Rosetta Stone software program. They often talked on the phone before they went on their trip, questioning why they weren't learning more important words. They learned about apples and bicycles, but some of the more basic words had yet to be taught. While in Italy, they had more than one experience where they had difficulty with the language. One day, they visited a bakery that had a glass case displaying the various pastries. Wayne asked about one that was called *La Mela*. John nearly fell over laughing. "La mela" means apple. In their phone calls, they had laughed often about the fact that one of the only words they had learned was apple, and here Wayne was asking what it meant.

One day when they were in need of cash, they went to the desk at the Hilton Condo complex where they were staying and asked for directions to the nearest ATM. The woman at the desk spoke English. She told them to turn right out of the driveway, go about two miles down the road, and look on their left for a big boot that was the advertisement for a shoe factory. The ATM was located across the street from the boot. John and Wayne drove up and down the road several times, but they never saw the boot. They stopped and conversed with some locals, trying to explain what they were looking for. They were saying things like "bank" and making gestures about putting a card into a slot and getting cash out. They were unsuccessful in getting anyone to understand and thought their miming would be hysterical to anyone who had seen it.

They returned to their wives with no cash. The next morning, they decided to try again. They were unsuccessful once more. They spotted a police officer, so they stopped and asked him. He said, "You want the *bancomat*," and then he pointed to a little awning in the shape of a semicircle. It was about 50 feet away. The ATM was so small compared to those in the U.S. that they had simply missed it. It actually looked like a payphone shelter. As they were using it, John happened to see the boot, which garnered a good laugh (trees had blocked their view from the road).

Finally it was time to leave Tuscany. John had arranged for a car service to take them back to Rome, where they were going to rent a car and drive to Sorrento, which would be their new base for exploring the Amalfi Coast. John had reserved a car with Avis, a company he had used for many years. When they got to the Avis counter, John showed the agent the printout of the Hilton Palace Hotel. The agent said he could just enter the address into the Garmin GPS and it would direct them to the hotel. This time, their car was much smaller, and it had a standard rather than an automatic transmission. John had not driven a standard in ages and was concerned about going up steep winding roads to get to Sorrento.

He went back to see if they had a larger car with an automatic transmission, but they did not. When they tried to program the hotel into the GPS, it didn't recognize it. John went back to the desk to ask for another unit, and the agent became skeptical and was visibly annoyed. He tried to program the address in, but he couldn't either. After failing with several more units, the agent said in a very nasty tone, "Just go to Sorrento. It is a small city. Ask when you get there." John was livid, but he went on his way. However, when he went to put the car in reverse, he couldn't find the gear because he was unfamiliar with the five-speed floor shift. This was enough to set Pat and Liz into laughter, some of it from nervousness about what was next. John took a deep breath and went back in to see the agent, who told him to press down on the gearshift and then move it left and forward. On the highway to Sorrento, John asked the girls to see if they could get Siri on their iPhones to provide directions to the hotel. To their amazement, after numerous missteps by the women, Siri found the hotel and provided flawless directions. They put the Garmin in the glove compartment and used Siri for the rest of the trip.

As they traveled along the winding, steep and narrow roads with no shoulder, they encountered what could only be called crazy Italians on two-seat motor scooters. The scooters were principally driven by young men, with their female passengers holding on to them. They would routinely come out into oncoming traffic and pull back into their own lane in the nick of time to avoid a head-on collision. It turned out that the day was an Italian holiday, and it seemed like every young person in Italy was on a motor scooter and they were all coming into John's lane.

Liz was oohing and aahing every time there was a close call. John told her it wasn't helpful for her to be doing that. It was stressful enough for him. He decided that he would keep to the legal speed limit, because there were so many cars behind him on the hills. Fortunately, they managed to get to Sorrento without an accident. By this time John had experienced enough driving, and they decided to take a bus to Amalfi, Ravello and Positano, which were their next stops. John and his copilot Wayne were so tense from driving that they consumed a lot of wine with dinner. They didn't stop there, but ordered several limoncellos after dinner. At midnight, the two men were on the balconies of their adjacent rooms singing the songs of Frankie Valli and the Four Seasons. Pat and Liz were sure they were going to be asked to leave the hotel, so they reined their husbands in for the night.

Pat and John had traveled a lot in their marriage and had many memorable moments. This trip was among the ones they would always remember. It's the good times they held onto when, less than two years later, they faced the biggest test of their lives.

CHAPTER 28

The Discovery

LIFE WAS HUMMING ALONG NICELY FOR THE Gamminos, but then came the day that would change their lives forever. In January of 2017, John and Pat were in the midst of remodeling their master bathroom in Vero Beach. The contractors were in the house taking measurements when Pat told John that she didn't feel well and was going to lie down. John said he would check on her in a few minutes. About five minutes later, Pat told John that her blood pressure was very high and her pulse was off the charts. While the neighbor rushed Pat to the emergency room at Indian River Medical Center, John asked the contractors to reschedule and raced to the ER himself.

Pat was taken in to have an X-ray of her heart area. The initial fear was that she had had a heart attack. They stabilized her and managed to get her blood pressure down and her pulse rate back to normal. There were, however, no enzymes in her bloodwork that would support a diagnosis of heart attack. The emergency room doctor came in and said that they had found a spot on Pat's lung and that a CT scan would be performed. The result showed that Pat had contracted lung cancer. The hospital pulmonologist, Dr. Velasquez, said a biopsy would have to be performed to confirm the diagnosis. John asked what stage he thought the cancer was in, and Dr. Velasquez said stage 3. Pat told John that she had known for a few weeks that she had a problem. She had gone to her personal physician for a respiratory issue, and he had done a chest X-ray. He told her there was a spot on her lung and that she should get in touch with an oncologist. She had kept it from John, who was shocked at the news.

Pat asked Dr. Velasquez' assistant how soon the biopsy could be scheduled. The woman said hopefully in the next few days. When Dr. Velasquez came back to show her the images of the CT scan, Pat also asked him about scheduling the biopsy. He responded, "This week, next week, what's the difference?" Pat and John were stunned by this cavalier and insensitive comment. Pat was eventually discharged and told to get in touch with her personal physician, Dr. Ron Williams. Dr. Williams referred her to Dr. Michael Layton, a pulmonologist who was very responsive and got her in quickly for the biopsy.

After the biopsy, Dr. Layton came out to talk to John, who had been waiting nervously. Dr. Layton said that Pat had non-small cell lung cancer, stage 3. John bravely asked, "How long does she have?"

Dr. Layton replied, "We hope for two good years." He said the oncologists would not be satisfied with that time frame, and they would do everything in their power to make it longer.

John was in shock. The love of his life since the age of 12 might have two years or less to live. On the ride home, John and Pat fought their tears but were not very successful.

During the next month, Pat met with a thoracic surgeon, an oncologist, a radiologist, a cardiologist and others. It was a rough month for the family, and John's mother, Rose, suffered a heart attack in the midst of it all. At one point Pat was on the third floor of the hospital and Rose was receiving treatment in the emergency room on the first floor. It was a harrowing time for John.

Through Dr. Layton, Pat was able to meet with Dr. Storey, an oncologist who had previously worked at MD Anderson Hospital in Houston, which was the number one hospital in the country for lung cancer treatment. Dr. Storey told Pat that she would have to undergo 37 radiation and eight chemotherapy treatments. He asked where she would like to have the treatments performed. Pat said at the Scully Welsh Cancer Center in Vero Beach. Pat and John toured the center courtesy of their friend Tom Lauda, who was on the foundation board there. It had state-of-the-art equipment and staff.

John had been researching various options for Pat, including taking her to MD Anderson in Houston. They also received advice from another oncologist, who advised Pat to find a good local hospital that could perform the treatments. She said that although the big hospitals have the great reputations, the initial treatments are standard. She said it would be better for Pat to be in the comfort of her home and surrounded by her friends and family. Otherwise she would have been in a hotel room in a strange city and all alone. It was great advice.

Scully Welsh Center had one of only four radiation machines in Florida. It cost $4 million and it was booked solid in 15-minute intervals. The machine was accurate to a fraction of a millimeter. The chemotherapy side of the center had individual rooms for each patient, and there were chairs for visitors and a curtain for privacy.

Pat had often said that if she were to get cancer, she would not go through the chemo and radiation treatments. However, at the insistence of her family who loved her so dearly, she agreed to do it. She had a wonderful relationship with Dr. Storey. He showed her much compassion, and he was attentive to John as well, since he knew that spouses suffer too in these situations.

Pat began radiation and chemotherapy treatments on February 24, 2017. Treatments ended on April 24. On May 1, she went for her first follow-up CT scan. Subsequently, she met with Dr. Peterson for her lab and imaging results and with Dr. Storey for the CT scan results. Both doctors were pleased with the results of the treatment. Dr. Storey said the cancer was virtually gone. He said many of the tumors had disappeared totally. Others had shrunk to a level below the threshold of concern. John and Pat were elated and most grateful. They discussed how lucky they were that she had had an outstanding physician and a wonderful place for her treatments.

In June, Pat had an MRI of her brain as a precaution, since lung cancer has a tendency to spread upward and not downward. The scan did not show any sign of the cancer moving to the brain. For three months, Pat and John enjoyed their lives. When they met with Dr. Storey after Pat's next scan, they were very relaxed and expecting continued good news. Unfortunately, that was not to be.

Dr. Storey said that the cancer had given the impression of being in remission, when in fact it had mutated to a different form of cancer known as EGFR, which stands for epidermal growth factor receptor. It was accompanied by a type of gene mutation that was a very aggressive form of lung cancer.

Pat and John were, of course, dejected after hearing the news. Dr. Storey said there was a new drug on the market that targeted this very strain of cancer and that he would prescribe it. It was called Tagrisso and it was manufactured by AstraZeneca.

Unfortunately, UnitedHealthcare would not approve the drug. They told Dr. Storey that Tagrisso was not a go-to drug.

Other drugs have to fail before a patient can try Tagrisso, because it is so expensive. Therefore, Dr. Storey prescribed a drug in a similar class, called Tarceva. After a short time, however, Pat's face began to break out, and she bled from dry skin. Her entire body was drying out, and she was becoming very upset. At her next appointment, she cried and told Dr. Storey that she would rather die than take that medicine. Dr. Storey consoled her and told her there were other options. He prescribed Opdivo, an immunotherapy drug. Pat tolerated it very well, but the next scan showed that it was not working and that the cancer had advanced.

Dr. Storey again prescribed Tagrisso. He didn't think the insurance company would have a problem with it since Pat had been on two other medications previously. However, Tagrisso was rejected again.

At this point John was beside himself and decided to take matters into his own hands. He sent an email to his golf group inquiring if anyone had a contact at AstraZeneca. He knew it was a long shot, but he did it anyway. His golf group had players from every walk of life, and among all their contacts there might be one that could help.

Sure enough, he received a call from Dick Patton, a member of the group. Dick said he knew a high-level executive at AstraZeneca — Bill Dwyer. Dick asked Bill if John could call him to discuss Pat's situation. Bill agreed, and during the phone call John explained the situation. Bill said he was pretty certain that his company could be of assistance.

Later that day, Bill called John and said his company had a program to help people like Pat. John was ecstatic, and filled out the necessary paperwork immediately. Within five days, Pat had Tagrisso on board, and it would be forthcoming from the manufacturer each month until the end of the year, when they would have to reapply.

Dr. Storey continued to monitor Pat's bloodwork every month, and they did imaging of her lungs every three months. The Tagrisso was working. It stopped the advance of the cancer and actually began shrinking the tumors. Pat seemed to tolerate the Tagrisso, though she suffered from dry skin all over her body (a known side effect). She addressed this with various creams. She looked great and was actually enjoying life with her friends and family.

In July of 2018, the family began its traditional week of vacation at Long Beach Island. They had rented a beautiful five-bedroom house with a swimming pool by the ocean. All was going well, but Pat's ankles swelled, and it made her very uncomfortable. Every morning, she got up to help prepare breakfast for the crew of 13. By late afternoon, she needed to lie down and take a short nap. Her family was very supportive, and every evening they got ice packs to place on her ankles. Nothing would stop Pat from laughing and enjoying her family. She likely knew this was the last time she would make it to the LBI vacation. She had been told that she might have 10 more months with the Tagrisso, based on its history of life extension.

During the trip, Pat and John also went to Phillipsburg. They stayed with friends from high school and enjoyed evenings out with other friends. All remarked on how good Pat looked. Less than a month later, Pat's health took a turn for the worse.

CHAPTER 29

The Shocking Turn of Events

IN AUGUST, PAT AND JOHN MADE THE DRIVE FROM New Jersey to Florida. A few days later, Pat came home from her mah-jongg game and told John that something very weird had happened. She had previously taught the other girls how to play the game, but this time she could not remember what to do. She couldn't remember what day it was either. John was very concerned, but she was speaking clearly and was able to relate what had happened without stumbling over her words. He wondered whether it might be a stroke, but decided she was lucid and maybe it was just a fluke.

The next morning, however, Pat was unable to function. John called Dr. Storey and was told to get her to the ER quickly. They immediately performed a CT scan. Pat had in fact had a stroke. It was called a "spray across the brain," and it inhibited her ability to speak. This incident led to further blood tests, swallowing tests and doctors' appointments. It also required that she go to speech therapy several times per week. Because of the stroke, Dr. Storey removed her from the Tagrisso until her symptoms improved. Tagrisso was known to have side effects that could aggravate cardiac problems. It was a delicate balance, since every day she was off the Tagrisso, the cancer was given a new opportunity to grow.

Pat was now seeing an oncologist, a neurologist, a pulmonologist, a thoracic surgeon, a cardiologist, a podiatrist and a gastroenterologist. John kept her schedule and drove her to each appointment. He gave up managing the golf group and also gave up golf. On September 27, Pat was feeling intense pressure around her heart and chest. John took her to the ER and they immediately ruled out a heart attack, but they found fluid around her right lung. The cancerous fluid was building up and causing the pressure. She would have to visit the pulmonologist to have it drained.

When they arrived for the appointment, Dr. Layton asked John if he had a weak stomach. If he had said yes, Dr. Layton was going to ask him to leave the room. John said he wanted to be present and could handle it. He watched as Dr. Layton penetrated Pat's back with a device connected to a tube that led to a bottle. The bottle was one liter in volume. The drainage process filled one bottle and three-quarters of a second one. Dr. Layton said that Pat would have to have a catheter put in for future drainage appointments.

The Grand Harbor community where Pat and John lived was incredibly supportive. Numerous women took turns in the morning keeping Pat company in the hospital or rehab facility to give John a break. On the evening the catheter was placed into Pat's side, two friends brought dinner to the house. They also brought a wonderful blanket with expressions of hope and love on it. Pat was feeling so unwell that she didn't want to see anyone or get out of bed. She only wanted to rest.

The next morning, October 3, John went in to wake Pat. She opened her eyes, but there was only a glaze present. She didn't seem to be focusing. John had watched Dr. Beristain, the neurologist, hold up his index finger and ask her to follow it as he moved it from side to side. John did the same, but Pat's eyes did not move. He called 911, and Pat was taken to the ER, where it was determined that she had had a second stroke. This one was debilitating to her left side. She would have to go into rehab and then have physical therapy, occupational therapy and speech therapy. It was an exceptionally difficult experience for both of them.

Pat was admitted to Encompass, a rehab facility, and the doctor's orders were for her to be drained every fourth day. The head nurse told John that the entire nursing staff was trained to perform the drainage procedure, and he was relieved. However, Pat was very upset when John arrived one morning. She said that a nurse had drained her during the night and hurt her. John went to the head nurse and told her that from then on, he wanted to be present when they drained her. Day or night, he would be there.

The next challenge that arose was when Pat needed to be drained on the third day in the cycle. Her nurse said he wouldn't do it, because the schedule was set for every four days. John said, "She is in pain, and she needs to be drained now."

The nurse refused. He was on one side of the bed, and John was on the other. John said he was going to the head nurse. The nurse said, "Don't bother. It won't get you anywhere." John wanted to punch him in the face, but he didn't want to put Pat's care in jeopardy.

He went outside to the head nurse, who reaffirmed the four-day schedule. John replied firmly, "She needs to be drained today. Are you going to call the doctor and get the orders changed, or am I? Your choice." She told John she would call the doctor to see what could be done. Five minutes later both the head nurse and the attending nurse came in to drain Pat.

John spoke to the doctors the next morning and asked them to please instruct the staff to drain her as needed. They agreed.

But that wasn't the end of it. One day a nurse came to perform the drainage, and she had a syringe and a pail. John went ballistic and explained that there was a specific kit for the drainage procedure. Again, he went to the head nurse. To John's amazement, the only staff member that was there that could drain her was the male nurse with whom he had had the confrontation. Recognizing that Pat was going to need this nurse, John apologized to him for being so angry.

Unfortunately, the difficulties continued. Pat's colon became bound up by the pain medication she was on. In an attempt to alleviate her suffering, the medical staff tried an enema and laxatives, to no avail. Therefore, they decided to administer colonoscopy medication. This was in the late evening, and John was worried about who the night nurse would be, and if it would be someone empathetic to Pat's situation. It turned out to be a 6-foot-4-inch male nurse. John was again upset at how insensitive the care was. She was going to be struggling with all these meds to initiate bowel movements, and it would be difficult enough to do that without the presence of a male nurse. John explained his concerns to the nurse. He asked for a female to help her when she had to go to the bathroom. The nurse seemed friendly and said he would make sure she got the care she needed.

John didn't sleep much that night. He went to the rehab center very early the next morning. Pat cried when she saw him, saying she didn't like the male nurse. He wasn't kind and caring but very matter-of-fact. He came in to give her medication but did not check on her. John asked if he had done anything to hurt her. She said no, but John wasn't sure she was telling the truth. He was livid with Encompass, and Pat never wanted to go there again. He told her she wouldn't and that she would be cared for at home. She was very relieved.

When Pat was released from rehab, arrangements were made for her to be cared for at home with VNA Hospice. She was scheduled for speech, occupational and physical therapy. A nurse came to bathe her three times a week. She was drained every morning. There was a parade of nurses and therapists in and out of the house each day. In their private moments, John would tell Pat that he would do anything for her. On trips to the bathroom, he told her never to be embarrassed about anything. While she was in her favorite position on the couch, he would kneel next to her and ask what she was thinking about. He tried to get her to tell him anything on her mind that she would like to share. Often, she would just cry. He would hold her and comfort her. Their love was incredibly strong. Often, no words were necessary. They both felt the bond of their beings together. Even at this stage, when John merely touched her to help her up, he would feel a stirring in his body. He loved her beyond words and beyond physical love. He adored her.

During this period, the family all pulled together and either Maureen, Melissa or Mike was always there to help. Pat's sisters, Mary Jane and Susan, also came to support her. Lisa cooked and left John with a freezer full of homemade soups. The Grand Harbor community rallied around them, and food was brought each day as friends and neighbors ensured that the family's meals were covered.

On November 14, Pat suffered her third stroke. This was a mild one without any new discernible damage to her speech or physical movement. She came home on November 16, and her sister Mary Jane came to help her and spend time with her. Pat seemed to be doing well. John washed her as he had done every day. He made sure she was dressed and her hair was brushed. However, at breakfast one morning, John noticed that she had a fork full of food and her hand was shaking. He saw her jaw drop. His heart pounded, and he dialed 911. She had had her fourth stroke. John followed the ambulance to the hospital and on the way called his brother. He told Jim, "This one was really bad, and I'm afraid it will do her in." Jim and his wife, Gina, raced from Orlando to Vero Beach to be with them. Maureen and Mary Jane came. The other family members hopped on planes and got there as soon as they could.

At the hospital, John met with the head surgeon of the stroke unit, who explained that the previous strokes had been sprays, and this one was a blockage. He said every minute they waited, more damage was occurring to the brain. The doctors were ready to operate, but they had to get in touch with Dr. Storey first. Pat's platelets were very low, and unless they could do a transfusion to get them from 25,000 to 55,000, they could not operate. The surgeon was having trouble reaching Dr. Storey, so John found the patient representative and borrowed her phone. He called Dr. Storey's office and explained that this was a life-and-death call. He asked for Dr. Storey to call the surgeon at the hospital, which he did immediately.

The two doctors spoke, and then Dr. Storey asked to speak with John. Dr. Storey advised John not to consent to the surgery, because Pat wouldn't survive it. John later realized that Dr. Storey was sparing him the pain and guilt of saying yes to an operation that would almost certainly result in Pat's death. Once the decision was made, Pat's family gathered around her. Father Dan Murphy from Holy Cross Church came to administer last rites. The last thing that Pat said before being transferred to the VNA Hospice facility was, "Who won the game?" She was a football fan until the end.

Pat was placed in a peaceful and quiet room that had a screened porch outside and a garden area, which was very nice for the family. John was asked how he wanted her to be treated. He said that he wanted her to be made comfortable. They understood and did as he asked. Pat was asleep for days.

The family all came to say their goodbyes. Children, grandchildren, sisters and friends came by each day to say goodbye. John was with her the entire time. He had told her he would be with her to the end. He slept in a chair by her bed every night. He held her hand and spoke softly to her, telling her how much he loved her. He told her what a wonderful wife and partner she was, and that she could go on her journey at any time. He whispered to her over and over. "It's okay to go. Just let me know that you are okay and save me a place next to you." One evening the entire family was gathered in her room and they prayed for her together. It was very touching.

On Thanksgiving Day, John ordered dinner for the family from the Grand Harbor Club. He knew that Pat would want them to celebrate Thanksgiving at the house as a family. They all wanted to stay with her, but they knew John was right about what Pat would want, so he stayed and they all went back to the house.

John had written a Thanksgiving prayer that he asked Michael to read before they had dinner at the house. Somehow his son summoned the strength to get through it.

A Thanksgiving Prayer

November 22, 2018

Dear Lord, we thank you for the wonderful family that is gathered here today to celebrate the Thanksgiving holiday. We have much to be grateful for. We are thankful to you for the good lives that you have provided us. We are thankful to you for the bountiful food and drink that we are about to enjoy on this special day. We pray for those less fortunate than us who are victims of poverty, war, terrorism and evil, and that they will find comfort in your promise of eternal life. We pray that you keep our military men and women safe as they protect our country and allow us to celebrate our blessings. And Lord, we pray that you will bless the special nurses and volunteers at VNA and VNA Hospice for the warmth, compassion and care that they provide to the sick and their families.

But Lord, on this particular Thanksgiving Day, we are grateful to you for giving us Patricia, our mother, grandmother, sister, wife and friend. We are grateful for the time that you have allowed us to share with her, to love her, to laugh with her and to cry with her. She has been an example and role model for all that have come to know her. She made many sacrifices in her life for us. She provided sunshine when there was darkness, laughter when there were tears, love when there was loneliness, caring when there was sickness and compassion when we needed a hug. We thank you for the special relationship that we share with each other that was nurtured by her. We are most grateful to you for giving us time with this beautiful woman who you are about to bring with you to her final resting place.

Lord, please help us to remember the good days, the good times, and the laughter we shared with her. As she embarks on this next leg of her journey, we pray that you will have mercy on her, and that she will enjoy peace and tranquility in the place you have prepared for her in heaven. And when our time comes to leave this world, we pray that you will save us a place next to her in your heavenly kingdom. We pray for these things in Jesus' name. Amen.

When dinner was over, the family came to see Pat and brought John a plate of food. The VNA nurses, who had seen death so many times, told John that Pat was close to leaving. John thought she would wait until after midnight so as not to have Thanksgiving always associated with her death. He stayed with her that night as he had for the duration of her stay there. He was afraid to leave the room for fear that she would leave while he was gone.

At 6:45 a.m. on Friday, November 23, the day after Thanksgiving, John was about to leave to go to the bathroom. As he looked at Pat, he saw that her eyes were open. He asked if she could see him, but she did not reply. Her eyes were fixed and her breathing was irregular. He pulled up a chair and held her hand. Again, he whispered that it was all right to go. He again asked her for two things: that she let him know she was okay, and that she save a place for him next to her.

At 7 a.m., Pat's breathing stopped. He kissed her and closed her eyes. Tears streamed down his face. He went for the nurse, who came in and pronounced that she was gone. She hugged John and said, "You did what you told her you would do. You stayed with her to the end." It was surreal. Pat and John had been together since seventh grade. They were 12 when they met, and their love was deep through good times and bad. Essentially, they had been together for 63 of their 75 years on the planet. They were married for 52 years. Now John had to tell the family that the woman they all loved so dearly was gone.

EPILOGUE

We live this life as individuals, but we also exist in the community that surrounds us. From the time we met, Pat and I enjoyed friendships in childhood, high school, college and the neighborhoods in which we lived. Some of those friendships remained with us throughout our lives.

When we moved to Vero Beach, Florida, we felt as though God had provided a slice of paradise. Due to the loving friends we found, we felt so lucky to have retired there. Pat was always a person who supported others in need. She gave selflessly of her energies to care for others. She fit well into the community where so many others were similarly inclined.

It would not be possible to relate all the good deeds that our friends and neighbors provided during Pat's sickness and particularly in her final weeks and days. Nor could I venture to thank everyone individually, knowing that I might inadvertently leave out someone special. From taking turns at the hospital and rehab centers to give me a break to providing meals for our family every night, the community banded together to show their love and heartfelt care. My family is forever grateful for the love and support that our friends provided.

Among the folks who should be considered saints are people at VNA and VNA Hospice. The consummate care that they provide is nothing short of wondrous. We had nurses parading in and out of our home to handle so many different aspects of Pat's comfort and care. We are in awe of their dedication.

The mores of the past have given way to new norms in our society. As the years have progressed, I have come to understand the decisions my father made that were literally life changing for Pat and me. He did what he thought was right at the time given his cognitive structure and what he thought was best for me. He was a tough guy and a veteran of World War II. He also lived through the Depression. As the years went by, he became mellow like most of us do, and was a wonderful grandfather to our children. He also loved and respected Pat for the many things she did for the family, particularly for him and my mother. I'm also happy to report that he and I developed a close friendship over the years.

Since Pat has been gone, I have begun a new and different journey into the world of writing books, songs and poetry. For a while there was such an emptiness and a need to find my center of gravity. It seemed hopeless at first. However, some very special people found their way into my life and the sun now fills much of the darkness that Pat left behind. I am now looking forward again to a new life of appreciation. One that focuses on what I have, and no longer on what I don't have. While Pat will always live in my heart, I have given myself permission to move on. I hope that those of you in similar circumstances can do the same.

LETTER TO THE READER

Dear Reader:

I hope that you enjoyed reading *The Love We Knew*. It is my very first book, and I wrote it because I felt compelled to share my family's story. I know that our trials are not unique, but I knew that telling these stories would bring comfort to those who had been through the same. The loss of Lisa at such a young age and the reunion nearly 20 years later was a very moving tale. I also want to make note of the fact that Pat was a true soldier in our journey from the pre-teen dating through our journey of 52 years of marriage. From giving up a baby for adoption to raising and supporting an extended family of 3 siblings, she rose to become a much-loved woman by so many people. She handled her final days with the graceful and quiet strength that described her adult years.

I would be most appreciative if you would leave a review on Amazon expressing your reaction to the book.

I also invite you to visit our website at johngammino.com, which will house my creative endeavors. Currently, there are three songs you can access through the site.

1. The Love We Knew
2. Wherever You Are
3. She's Nobody's Woman

"The Love We Knew" is a song with the same title as the book. It is a song of remembrance for those who have lost a loved one.

"Wherever You Are" is a song of encouragement. It describes the things that occurred after Pat left this dimension of life and moved to another. Nearly all the events described in the song, and the video that is also available, happened.

"She's Nobody's Woman" was my attempt to write a song in an entirely different genre. It tells a story of a free-spirited woman who lives in the moment.

I hope that you will find the songs enjoyable and that you will download them from one of the sites that hosts them. Thank you again for reading our story.

John

ABOUT THE AUTHOR

JOHN GAMMINO had an immensely successful 50-year career in the business world. For 17 years, he served in top-level management positions for one of the largest telecom companies in the U.S. In 1984, he bravely formed his own consulting firm and for the next 30 years logged significant accomplishments for 150 clients, including telecom giants, government agencies, investment firms and law firms. These days his top priorities are his family, his golf game, and his writing, which includes song lyrics and very likely another book.